HOLLYWOOD NOW

HOLLYWOOD NOW

By William Fadiman

Foreword by Irving Wallace

LIVERIGHT   NEW YORK

1.98765432
International Standard Book Number: 0-87140-556-3
Library of Congress Catalog Card Number: 72-87097

Manufactured in the United States of America

For

JOHN ALFRED LESSER

whose idea it was

An incalculable debt of gratitude and love—since she happens to be my wife—is owed by the writer to Dr. Regina K. Fadiman, whose editorial criticism, suggestions, recommendations, and judicious guidance were of inestimable aid in the writing of this book from its inception to its termination.

A very small portion of the material in these pages has appeared in other forms in *The Saturday Review* and *The New Republic*.

CONTENTS

FOREWORD

I remember clearly the first time I set eyes upon William Fadiman, the author of this book. It was in January of 1950, and for me it was a memorable occasion.

I had been struck by a unique idea for a motion picture —the story of four young women, friends because their four husbands were in the same bomber crew in Korea, who were all widowed on the same day when their husbands' plane was shot down. The lone survivor of the fatal crash, a bachelor, comes into their lives with last words or effects from their husbands, which helps resolve the shattered lives of the widows. I wrote this as a thirteen page original story meant to be a motion picture. Only because I was broke and could not afford to write the story as a novel or play had I decided to prepare it as a movie original. But submitting the story in that form meant the odds of selling it were heavily against me.

To clarify this for the uninitiated, I can do no better than to quote from Chapter 5 in this book. "The film industry does everything in its power to discourage 'originals,'" writes

William Fadiman. "This discouragement begins with the stories purchased for the screen. The industry concentrates on
story material which has already attained recognition
through prior publication or, in the case of a play, prior
production. This practice, of course, eliminates any serious
consideration of 'originals,' for they have had no such public
exposure or testing. Hollywood is afraid—and this is only
one of its many fears—afraid to trust its own judgment or
even its own experience."

This was as true in January of 1950 as it is today. But
fortunately, in 1950 there were a few persons working in the
film studios who were not afraid to trust their judgment of an
untested manuscript—and Fadiman was one of these.

When I had completed my thirteen page story, entitled
A Young Wives' Tale, my agents decided not only to submit
it to the story departments of the major studios but to arrange for me to meet an executive at each studio and elaborate upon the brief story orally, in the hope that this might
help overcome the odds against selling originals.

One of the first studio executives I was taken to meet
was Fadiman, a well-known but awesome figure who was
installed at RKO-Radio Pictures in Hollywood as the Executive Assistant to the legendary and invisible Howard Hughes,
owner of the studio.

I knew a little about Fadiman's background before I met
him. For fourteen years, first in New York and then in Culver
City, California, he had been the powerful Scenario and
Story Editor for Metro Goldwyn Mayer, counseling Louis B.
Mayer on which scenarios should be made into films and
what literary material should be purchased. Then, when
Dore Schary moved over to RKO-Radio Pictures to run that
studio, he hired Fadiman as his Executive Assistant in charge
of stories, writers, and various aspects of film production.
Later, after Howard Hughes had acquired RKO and Schary

had departed, Hughes retained Fadiman as his personal Executive Assistant. Incidentally, Hughes visited the motion picture studio he had purchased only once. He came by night, wandered around the lot, and as he was about to leave he was asked if he had anything to say about his acquisition. "Yes," said Hughes. "Paint it."

And so, that afternoon in 1950, I found myself seated across from the man Hughes had selected to advise him on story material that might translate well into motion pictures. Somewhat nervously I narrated to Fadiman what he had already read in my thirteen pages. He sat somberly, thoughtfully, through my recital and made notes. When I was out of breath, and finished, he began to pepper me with questions about my characters and plot line and certain possible scenes. The questions were pertinent, and they stimulated me to verbalize many ideas that I had not put on paper.

At last, I was done.

Suddenly, Fadiman smiled, a warm full smile. "It's a great story," he said. "Absolutely wonderful. I love it. I'm positive it'll make a fascinating motion picture. As far as I'm concerned, we'd like to buy it. There is only one more step. I'll need Howard Hughes' approval. I'll pass it on to him with my recommendation. We'll have to wait until we hear from him."

Then Fadiman turned to one of my agents, who had accompanied me, and said, "It may take a little time hearing from Mr. Hughes. If you get another offer right away, don't sell the story without letting me know. I'd want to know, and push Mr. Hughes for a decision if I have to, because I want *A Young Wives' Tale* for RKO."

I left the studio airborne, walking on clouds. Fadiman had entered my private pantheon of the wisest men on earth.

Several days later we did get an offer, from Metro Goldwyn Mayer. My agent notified Fadiman at RKO at once. Desperately, Fadiman tried to locate Howard Hughes. He was unable to do so in the time allotted him. And so the story was sold to MGM.

But this was not the end of my relationship with William Fadiman. Exactly two years after that introductory meeting I had my second meeting with him, and it was more successful than the first. I had written an eighty-three page original story for films entitled *Split Second*. It was about a killer-thief on the run, who takes a varied group of hostages for self-protection and hides out in an abandoned shack in the Nevada desert awaiting the arrival of a colleague in crime. What the killer doesn't know, and later refuses to believe, is that he and his hostages are hiding out on an atomic-bomb test range near Las Vegas, and that a nuclear bomb is to be detonated at dawn. Well, Fadiman loved that story even more than the first one. He, and a producer whom he had interested in the original, recommended its purchase to Howard Hughes. After months of waiting, Hughes responded. "Buy it."

So Fadiman bought *Split Second* for RKO and hired me to adapt it into a screenplay. Eventually, it was made into a film—the first directorial effort by Dick Powell—starring Alexis Smith, Stephen McNally, Jan Sterling. It was a success at the box office; Fadiman's judgment had proved sound.

About a year later, Fadiman became a producer at Columbia Pictures, and hired me to work with Jerome Weidman in adapting a Horace McCoy novel for the screen.

In the months of working at RKO and at Columbia studios, I saw Fadiman almost daily. I learned much about him, and he a good deal about me. I learned that he had graduated from the University of Wisconsin, had made Phi Beta Kappa, and had attended the Sorbonne. In his youth he had been a writer, a literary critic for New York's newspapers and magazines. He had been General Manager of the Leland

Hayward agency before joining Metro Goldwyn Mayer in the East, and then had come on to Hollywood. Fadiman learned from me that I had always written for magazines and was now writing for films as a prelude to writing novels. I enjoyed some parts of screen writing, but I disliked adapting the work of others, and I hated the whole Hollywood concept of writing by committee. I wanted to get out and write on my own, without an employer hovering over me. Fadiman constantly encouraged me to break free, despite the financial risk. He had respect for the printed word, for individual creativity, and a love of the book, especially the honest one.

In 1959 I finally did break free of the studios and wrote a novel, *The Chapman Report*. When it was submitted for motion picture consideration, Fadiman was at Columbia Pictures and he immediately recommended that the studio buy the film rights. Nine studios and production companies submitted bids for the novel, and ultimately it was sold to the Darryl F. Zanuck corporation and produced.

But long before that, out of mutual respect and affection, out of intellectual things held in common and emotional experiences shared, Bill Fadiman and I had become friends. Our professional relationship ended, as he continued to rise in the film industry and I removed myself from Hollywood and went off to write novels, but our social relationship continued. I watched him go on from Columbia Pictures to Seven Arts Productions, where he was Vice President for six years. I saw him become Executive Literary Adviser at Warner Brothers–Seven Arts. And finally, I saw him expand his activities into the area he had always loved most of all— that of the printed word.

I was among the many who, during that time, attempted to persuade Fadiman to write about his own field. Few men I had met knew as much about every aspect of the Hollywood scene and motion-picture-making as he did. He had been in demand at colleges, various organizations, and writers' gatherings to lecture on the art of the cinema. Still, along with his other friends, I felt it should be set down on paper. And then to our delight Bill did begin putting articles and essays on paper, pieces on Hollywood that appeared in the *Los Angeles Times, Saturday Review, Frontier, The New Republic, Films and Filming,* and other publications.

Not enough, we said. What was really wanted was a book about Hollywood and movie-making. There had been many good ones, but they were not telling the real story, and we felt that only Bill had the knowledge, insight, and overall perspective to write a definitive inside book on every aspect of motion-picture-making and the movie community.

The result of his efforts is the most thorough and honest book yet written on Hollywood and movie-making, written as Fadiman had known it for thirty years, and as he knows it today. And here it is.

I think it is important for readers to know what it is and is not. The book is not a routine history of Hollywood or film-making. It is not a book of gossip about movie personalities. It is not a how-to-do manual on the technique of making a motion picture. True, of necessity, it contains a little of each of those elements, but it is not devoted exclusively to any one of them. Nor is this book a superficial puff about Hollywood and its wonder-workers. Fadiman seeks to tell the truth.

I am reminded of the occasion when Wilson Mizner, a gambler, wit, and playwright, was brought into a courtroom on some charge or other. During the proceedings, the judge said angrily, "Are you trying to show contempt of court?" To which Mizner replied, "No, Your Honor, I am trying to conceal it." I would say this is fairly much Fadiman's approach to his handling of Hollywood. He makes an effort to be understanding and objective, even if critical, about the culture of the natives he has known so well.

Fadiman could have written a sensational book about Hollywood. He certainly has the ammunition, and it would have been an easier book to write. I've often heard him relate his incredible experiences with headline movie personalities. I recall his speaking of Howard Hughes, "who always met me at three or four in the morning for our conferences, meetings that took place away from the studio at some unmarked office building to which I was taken via three separate cars which awaited me at various locations." I recall his speaking of Elizabeth Taylor and Richard Burton, "who offered me a drink and rolled a liquor cart in from their bedroom which was its permanent abode, and the conversation afterwards was limited to a discussion of 17th century poetry." I recall his speaking of one famous studio head, "who called me at 9:15 one morning and asked that a one-page synopsis—no longer—of *War and Peace* be on his desk by 11 o'clock that same morning. I did it, but Tolstoi has never been the same to me since." I recall his speaking of the time when he unpacked a huge crate containing an unedited manuscript entitled *Gone with the Wind* and of how he had to tell the story of that novel "to the chairman of my company while he was ill in bed with a severe cold, a telling continuously interrupted by his coughing and sneezing, and then he informed me at the end of my rendition that the book was too sad, that too many people died, that nobody wanted to see a picture about the Civil War, and that it would never attract a book-buying public anyway."

Delightful as all that is, it takes much more than anecdotage to produce a comprehensive, useful book about Hollywood, one such as Fadiman has written. For mere frivolity, one must go elsewhere. But despite my years in and around Hollywood, until I read this book I lacked a complete picture of how Hollywood—especially The New Hollywood— works and lives and thinks. Meaning how The Agent, The Director, The Star, The Writer, The Producer function.

In these pages the reader will discover why Hollywood's "former oligarchic empire shattered and fragmented," and will learn details of the present power structure, the great conglomerates, "a faceless, impersonal, remote power" which "now dominates a historically individualistic industry." The reader will meet for the first time—introduced in no other previous book on movies, to my knowledge, with this kind of insight—The Agent, whom Fadiman considers "unquestionably the most significant individual in Hollywood's galaxy of personalities." I would say that this chapter alone is worth the price of admission.

His narrative should have, I would guess, enormous appeal to four kinds of readers: those who've read or heard about Hollywood, enjoyed its product on television and in theaters, and are curious to know the truth about how the strange and wonderful city of celluloid and tape really operates; those who intend to come to Hollywood as visitors or spectators and who want a guidebook that will reveal to them what goes on behind the façades; those who plan to come to Hollywood in hope of working in the motion picture industry; and, finally, those who are interested in making films of their own, anywhere, and who want to know how films are really made by the professionals in what remains the world's most renowned center of motion picture production.

For all those readers, William Fadiman's book will be not only an entertainment but an education.

IRVING WALLACE

HOLLYWOOD NOW

HOLLYWOOD

Farthest from any war, unique in time
Like Athens or Baghdad, this city lies
Between dry purple mountains and the sea.
The air is clear and famous, every day
Bright as a postcard, bringing bungalows
    And sights. The broad nights advertise
For love and music and astronomy.

Heart of a continent, the hearts converge
On open boulevards where palms are nursed
With flare-pots like a grove, on villa roads
Where castles cultivated like a style
Breed fabulous metaphors in foreign stone,
    And on enormous movie lots
Where history repeats its vivid blunders.

Alice and Cinderella are most real.
Here may the tourist, quite sincere at last,
Rest from his dream of travels. All is new,
No ruins claim his awe, and permanence,
Despised like customs, fails at every turn.
    Here where the eccentric thrives,
Laughter and love are leading industries.

Luck is another. Here the body-guard,
The parasite, the scholar are well paid,
The quack erects his alabaster office,
The moron and the genius are enshrined,
And the mystic makes a fortune quietly;
    Here all superlatives come true
And beauty is marketed like a basic food.

O can we understand? Is it ours,
A crude whim of a beginning people,
A private orgy in a secluded spot?
Or alien like the word harem, or true
Like hideous Pittsburgh or depraved Atlanta?
    Is adolescence just as vile
As this its architecture and its talk?

Or are they parvenus, like boys and girls?
Or ours and happy, cleverest of all?
Yes. Yes. Though glamorous to the ignorant
This is the simplest city, a new school.
What is more nearly ours? If soul can mean
    The civilization of the brain,
This is a soul, a possibly proud Florence.

KARL SHAPIRO

THE INDUSTRY

Some wag remarked bitterly, in the early days of tele-
vision, that TV in two years had arrived at a mediocrity
that radio had taken a quarter of a century to achieve. The
same cannot be said of the movies. The ambitious struggle
to achieve an audience made up exclusively of children has
been long and arduous. It has been over such resisting
bodies as Chaplin and Garbo and Goldwyn and Lubitsch,
even Walt Disney. But the heights have been won.

ROBERT ARDREY

Although the ensuing chapters in this book will explore in
detail the activities and roles of The Agent, The Director,
The Star, The Writer, and The Producer, all major partici-
pants in the making of films, it seems advisable to present
first a portrait of the film industry as a whole. With this as a
background, the reader may be better able to understand
these various functionaries as individuals and as interrelated
contributors to the industry. And assuredly, Hollywood,
jolted as it has been from its former throne of complacency
to its current frightened and confused status, needs a reas-
sessment of its whole as well as its parts.

Hollywood has been described as a warm Siberia, Poughkeepsie with Palms, Baghdad-on-the-Pacific, a carnival without concessions, and, by Raymond Chandler, as "a world with the personality of a paper cup." Still, most of its residents would agree on one point: Hollywood used to be a pleasant place in which to work and live, and its rewards were bounteous. No more. Hollywood in the seventies is irresolute, apprehensive, divided, and plagued with problems. In its sixty-year history Hollywood has endured numerous setbacks, but at no other period has its survival been so threatened. Fear is an unwelcome, unbidden guest at the dinner tables in Beverly Hills, Bel Air, the Trousdale Estates, and San Fernando Valley.

Hollywood's former oligarchy has been broken up, its once monolithic studio structure splintered into dozens of small companies and individual units. It is being assailed from every side: the death or abdication of the great moguls of the past, the increase in "runaway" films (American-financed productions manufactured outside of the United States), a loss of customers from the mounting appeal of television, a dissatisfaction with its censorship code, and competition from foreign films. Desperate and frustrated, Hollywood has put up a For-Sale sign and an unexpected buyer has been found in "the conglomerates," the industrial behemoths which now dominate American business. Their incursion may well be the final deadly weapon leveled at Hollywood's dream castles.

Having succeeded in such disparate ventures as real estate, garages, metals, chemicals, insurance, and communications, Big Business saw no reason why investment in films might not be equally profitable. But thus far the new industrial overseers have found themselves incapable of dealing effectively with their new giant toys. The film community has defied their most determined, businesslike efforts to cope with its creative vagaries and eccentric personnel. The conglomerates have been unable to organize and control Hollywood's sprawling, amorphous dominion. The owners of the New Hollywood have discovered to their dismay that creativity cannot be calibrated. They cannot understand a business which is at the same time an art and an industry.

It is not necessary to examine the specific reasons why the conglomerates infiltrated Hollywood at the lowest ebb in its fortunes. These reasons involve a bizarre combination of business acumen and a naive fascination with show business, which is actually a form of being screenstruck. It is enough to know that the motion picture industry still has enormous assets and potentialities. The assets are millions of dollars worth of real estate and thousands of copyrights on story material, such as books and plays, as well as those on old films and music. Neither of these, however, have anything to do with the making of motion pictures except as collateral capital resources.

Before exploring the impact and influence of the conglomerates, it might be well to examine the Hollywood they acquired, the film industry as it is today. What did the New Hollywood inherit from the Old Hollywood? What events, dilemmas, and disasters brought Hollywood to such a vulnerable state as to permit its purchase by these alien lords of finance? What did the conglomerates actually buy?

Let us begin by admitting that there is no such thing as Hollywood anymore except as a geographic place name. If there were a film capital today, it would not be Hollywood, with the Motion Picture Relief Fund announcing in April 1970 the existence of a "crisis . . . a tragic unemployment situation coupled with the increasing needs of those out of work." It would not be Hollywood, where the famous Hollywood Studio Club, a housing haven for almost fifty years for thousands of ambitious young women seeking careers in films, has announced its closing for lack of funds. It would not be Hollywood, where there was so little work available for extras from January to June 1970 that many did not work the 160 hours required to make them eligible for the health and welfare benefits provided by the Screen Extras Guild. It would not be Hollywood, with its dozens of empty stages and over 42 percent of its normal work force thronging the unemployment insurance lines of Van Nuys, Santa Monica, and Los Angeles. "There's no question about it," said the *Los Angeles Times* of March 17, 1971, in its lead editorial:

> *If the economy as a whole is in a recession, the motion picture business—in terms of films produced here rather than abroad—is in an out-and-out depression. More than half of the 30,000 local film union members are out of work. In some crafts, joblessness is said to be running 85% to 90%.*

And Mel Shavelson, President of the Writer's Guild of America, West, was quoted by *Variety* of March 16, 1971, as follows:

> *Suddenly, the whole face and temper of our town has changed. The laughter is a little uneasy, the humor has turned black, and we are in the grip of a change like no other we have witnessed before.... The giants have gone and in their place we have the dodgers. Our town is facing the bleakest year in recent memory. The town itself, the collection of artists and craftsmen who have made Hollywood unique in the world, is slowly breaking up. And no one is really doing anything about it.*

A swift summary and appraisal of the staggering losses endured by the major companies in the first years of this decade, almost coincidental with the arrival of the conglomerates in Hollywood, is disheartening. Twentieth Century Fox reported a 1970 loss of $77,335,000, and a pre-tax loss in 1969 of $65,257,000. The loss sustained by Metro Goldwyn Mayer for 1969 was $71,937,000, and $16,723,000 for 1970—the great decrease resulting not from higher box-office revenues but from the income from the forced sale of real estate and other studio owned assets. The final figure for 1970 on the financial performance of United Artists—long lauded by Wall Street as the one company of substance and stability because its income was not eroded by the ownership of a studio—revealed an after-tax net loss of $45,480,000. Universal, largely because of its studio tours for visitors (a million dollar annual business) emerged with a very slight profit, but by far the lowest it has recorded for years. Paramount wrote off huge deficits in 1969 and 1970, and though blessed in 1971 with the revenues from *Love Story*, the President of Gulf and Western, Paramount's conglomerate owner, announced in April 1971 that "write-downs on other Paramount movies that have lost money would offset the profits from this one picture." This in itself is an illuminating comment on the state of the industry—that a picture predicted to gross more than $100 million, which cost $2.2 million, cannot prevent its sponsoring studio from registering a deficit. The truth about Warner Brothers' operations is embedded in the overall statements of its conglomerate proprietor, Kinney National Services; but Kinney's annual report did not conceal the fact that of all its various units, the film company was the least remunerative. The largest of the non-major film organizations, National General, recorded a loss of $5,060,000 in 1970 before taxes. Columbia Pictures' loss for fiscal 1971 was $28,772,000, the largest in its history, and it promptly cancelled a semi-annual 3 percent stock dividend. It has been estimated by *Variety* that the combined losses of all major companies in the three-year period ending in 1971 could be close to $600,000,000. 1972 has seen the emergence of a few successful pictures, among them one box-office smash, *The Godfather*. But welcome though it is, one swallow does not make a summer.

There was a time in the history of Old Hollywood, especially during the forties, often referred to as the Golden Period, when all film companies expected and frequently derived profits from their pictures that seemed almost preposterous when compared to any other business in the world. Incredible as it seems, there were a number of pictures made during that period which returned as much as sixteen hundred percent on the investment. How are the mighty fallen!

There has been a precipitous decline in the total number of annual productions. During 1969 and 1970 the number of feature films initiated in America and abroad by major American companies slumped by nearly 34 percent. In 1936 there were 763 films released in America; in 1946 there were 425; in 1970 there were only 232. And this alarming reduction in the quantity of films took place during a period of fantastic population growth.

In addition to facing shattering contractions in revenue, Hollywood is now also coping with unprecedented cost increases, which might have been absorbed in periods of prosperity (meaning high audience attendance), but are now a serious burden. According to the Motion Picture Association of America, the average expenditure for an individual picture has risen by over 50 percent since 1961. The amounts paid for stories, the price of film, the fees for advertising and exploitation, the cost of prints, the payment to performers, producers, writers, directors, and executives, and most onerous of all, the heightened wage-scales of the numerous union-protected craftsmen and technicians needed to mount a film —all have increased. And this stupendous cost rise has not been compensated for by a commensurate advance in ticket prices (10 cents in 1930; $3.00 in 1971), though box-office patrons may think otherwise. Nor is there any evidence of a larger number of film-goers. In other words, Hollywood is making fewer pictures for fewer viewers at a greater cost per picture.

This does not mean that film production has come to a halt, but Hollywood is no longer the place where the majority of American-sponsored films are being manufactured. American films are being made all over the world, and in a hundred cities and villages in America itself. Hollywood has moved from Burbank, Culver City, and Gower Street to Rome, London, Shanghai, New York, and Burning Stump, Arkansas, or Meddling Ditch, Kentucky. Itinerant producers set up shop wherever the locale and the economic advantages can be enjoyed most profitably. "A rock is a rock, a tree is a tree. Shoot it in Griffith Park" is no longer valid.

These productions made outside of Hollywood have come to be known as "runaway films," and by far the greatest percentage of them are being produced overseas. The figures speak for themselves. In 1968 there were 232 films created by Americans, of which 123 were made outside the United States. In 1969 there were 226 American-sponsored films, of which 118 were not produced in this country. Of the 237 American films in 1970, almost 100 were manufactured abroad. Seven out of every ten films shown in the United States are in this "runaway" category, whereas in the late 1950s only 5 percent of the feature films produced by American-owned or American-financed companies were initiated and completed outside our borders. Of the 181 available sound stages in Hollywood, only 65 to 70 were active in 1970.

A principal reason for making pictures away from Hollywood can be found in the staggering rise in local wages and salaries on every level of film-making. Nurtured by past prosperity, caught in the grip of inflation, the unions which represent the majority of Hollywood's technicans have done little to relax their working demands or to lower salary stipulations in order to make producing in Hollywood more feasible. Union officers are fully cognizant of the growing defection by producers seeking greener pastures, and of the economic harm this is doing their members; but beyond publicizing Hollywood's plight with the slogan, "repatriation or ruin," their efforts to preserve Hollywood have been insubstantial and ineffective. Such minor concessions as they have granted apply largely to low-budget pictures and are not sizeable enough to compete satisfactorily with the lower labor costs outside Hollywood. Donald P. Haggerty, business representative of the film technician's union and vice-president of the Hollywood Film Council, put it simply in the *Los Angeles Times* in March 1971 when he said, "We just can't compete financially."

Haggerty is right. Inasmuch as a large proportion of the budget of a film is allocated for labor, it is obvious why it is financially more advantageous to make a picture where wages are low, and where the salaries paid extras, for example, are not governed by unions as they are in Hollywood. It is even more beneficial abroad where co-productions with foreign nationals aided by government subsidies offer a saving of approximately 15 percent to American producers. Hollywood has never found a way to counter this. It is doubtful whether the conglomerates will be any more successful.

The new rajahs of Hollywood have been forced to accept the "runaway" film concept purely for self-protection. So the producer who opts to shoot away from Hollywood is usually given grudging approval by his bosses. That they do this with reluctance is understandable, for though foreign production decreases the cost of the films, it also leaves the companies with partially or completely empty studios, the maintenance costs of which often more than offset the gains made by the lower production charges. The expense involved in keeping a Hollywood studio open and available for full-scale production is devastating; even a non-operating studio requires a number of permanent employees, payments for insurance, security measures, and other fixed fees and costs totalling approximately $100,000 a week.

The ever increasing salaries paid to stars are another burden. Actors are aware of the economic crisis in the industry and some have modified their stipulations and demands. But such accommodations are relatively minor in the overall expense patterns, and they are usually applied to low-budget films which rarely use stars anyway. The prodigious sums demanded by many stars have given rise to the suggestion (implemented on occasion) that high-budget films be made without any stars at all. Since stars have been the foundation stones of Hollywood, this proposal is startling, for the star system is Hollywood's most sacrosanct institution. To seriously consider jettisoning it is a dramatic index of the gravity of Hollywood's current condition and the desperation of its new conglomerate owners.

The salaries paid to screenwriters, now augmented by what they receive from the sale of their films to television, add to the financial problems of the studios. Directors and producers, too, receive high salaries and also participate more and more frequently in the profits of their films, making a further drain on corporate resources. Thus far, the New Hollywood has not proposed to eliminate these three vital contributors, as it *has* suggested ending the star system. Instead, it has tried to combine their functions wherever possible, thus effecting modest savings. The effects of this somewhat radical revision in the chain of command in the making of a motion picture will be discussed later.

But the major problem confronting Hollywood is the persistent reduction in the quantity of its patrons. In 1969 15 million Americans went to the movies weekly as against 87 million in 1957, a significant date, because it was before the advent of television. At a conference held at the University of Southern California in March 1971, Gordon Stulberg,

President of Twentieth Century Fox and a veteran film executive, advised his listeners that "The number of paid film admissions in the United States this year will be the lowest in the history of the movie business since the advent of sound."

What was once a movie-going habit has become an occasion, which tends to benefit two kinds of films: those receiving extraordinary publicity through shrewd and expensive exploitation; and those of a highly libidinous or pornographic nature—a type that is fast losing its appeal because of the films' lack of invention, their tedious similarity, and their overt repetitiousness. But these two seem to be the only varieties of film which will tempt the ordinary movie-goer to leave the comfort of his home TV and travel to a neighborhood cinema. Rising costs, fewer films, and runaway productions are bad enough; but practically empty theaters are intolerable. A product without a market, or at best one that is shrinking rapidly, is a doomed product. The lifeline of Hollywood is the length of the queue in front of the box office.

What makes people go to the movies? This has become a prime question for investigation by the new conglomerate owners. Who determines what the film-goers will want to see? Who is responsible? Is it the studio head, functioning through his producers, who rules initially on the selection of the film, or is he merely an echo of the tastes and desires of the public he is trying to please?

There are people both inside and outside of the industry who believe that the majority of Hollywood films are simply a mirroring of public taste and that Hollywood merely complies with the demands of that public. This viewpoint is epitomized in the comment of Adolph Zukor, one of the founders of Paramount Pictures and an extremely successful film-maker, who tailored all his company's productions to his conviction that "The public is never wrong." Jack Valenti, President of the Motion Pictures Association of America, agrees: "The movie is a reflector and not an innovator." On that premise, Hollywood merits neither praise nor blame for its films; the only adjudication to be made is one based on its ability to reproduce accurately what it believes are public mandates. This avoidance of any obligation or accountability goes hand in hand with Hollywood's stubborn belief that the mind of the average American film-goer is that of a twelve-year-old child.

In his *Hollywood: The Movie Colony—The Movie Makers*, Leo Rosten notes that:

> *The movie makers are in many ways compelled to feed a popular diet to a public which is in firm possession of deplorable tastes—tastes derived from sources far older, deeper, and more potent than Hollywood. The very success of Hollywood lies in the skill with which it reflects the assumptions, the fallacies, and the aspirations of an entire culture. The movie producers, the movie directors, the movie writers and the movie actors work with the stereotypes which are current in our society— for they, too, are children of that society; they, too, have inherited and absorbed the values of our world. But Hollywood, through the movies, reenforces our typologies on an enormous scale and with overpowering repetitiveness. Whether the movies imitate life or whether life imitates the movies is for others to decide. . . . Some critics say that audiences complain about the movies because the movies do not reflect reality; it is this writer's suspicion that more people lament the fact that reality does not reflect the movies. (Underscoring mine.)*

One might assume that Hollywood would have a consuming interest in this controversy over the origin and derivation of its films, but such was not the case in the Old Hollywood of the tycoon owners nor is it in the New Hollywood of the conglomerates. Its concern seems to be only in the audience response to its productions, not in the reasons for that response. If the studio heads were able to prophesy audience reactions they would happily do so, but this is not possible. The most astute executive in Hollywood's hierarchy cannot determine in advance, no matter what he may say publicly or think privately, whether the film he is preparing will meet with approval, derision, or be totally ignored—the worst fate of all. The audience's potential response to a film is an unknown and always will be, surveys, polls, and analyses to the contrary. But whether the films we see reflect the collective consciousness of the public or are solely the product of the producer's personal taste and inclinations, the despairing fact remains that the audiences for an unprecedentedly large percentage of Hollywood films are getting smaller and smaller. This has never happened before in the sixty-year history of Hollywood. Nor do the new owners of the industry seem to be able to do anything about it.

Once upon a time audiences were composed of people who went to the movies to see anything; there was little discrimination on Movie Nights. As patrons became more sophisticated they also became more selective, so that today they no longer go to *the* movies, they go to *a* movie. While the mediocrity of Hollywood films is certainly a factor in this greater selectivity, another element affecting film patronage has come into being—the emergence of a new, young audience. Today 62 percent of all movie-goers are between twelve and thirty years of age. This has prompted the New Hollywood to make frantic efforts to woo this new audience by making films expressly for it. But again and again the studios find that as a collective group it is unpredictable, disloyal, extraordinarily fragmented, "and probably less forgiving than any critic alive," to quote Charles Champlin from the *Los Angeles Times* of April 23, 1972. Thus far, it has rebelliously defied the development by Hollywood of any commercially viable pattern of film entertainment which would insure the unflagging devotion of its disparate members or even sustain their enthusiasm for any specific type of film-making. Various formulas have been tried, have achieved short-lived triumphs, and then been abandoned.

While engaged in this effort to capture the youth market, the film companies have been attacked on another flank. In the course of concentrating their business and creative energies on pleasing youth, they have almost completely ignored the family unit. It is incontestable that making films uniquely or mainly for the young has alienated what was once the bulk of the American motion picture audience, the middle-aged father with his wife and children, once habitual movie-goers. Nowhere is the generation gap so apparent, for the family unit has rejected the contemporary film as entertainment, and box-office revenue from the youth group in no way compensates for the absence of millions of dollars which once streamed in steadily from family patronage.

And so, as Pauline Kael has observed in *The New Yorker*, "Most movies these days are made for nobody; the proportion of movies that fail commercially is at an all-time high, and now when they fail they often fail mercilessly— sometimes on the opening day of a first-run movie a theatre does not sell a single ticket—so that investing money in movies is becoming a fantastic long-shot gamble against public apathy." It is this world of the "fantastic long shot" that the new owners have embraced, a world they never made.

On television, of course, different tastes can be gratified by turning a dial. Wryly enough, movies are among the most favored programs on TV. Mutilated and distorted though they are by conscienceless editing and the arbitrary insertion of commercials, they are watched by millions at home. Why pay for a film when you can see it for nothing? Thus, whereas only 15 million Americans attend the movies once a week, 135 million see television daily in 56 million homes, and a high percentage of these viewers are looking at movies made in Hollywood. Motion pictures consume 15 percent of what Madison Avenue dubs prime time, and the figure is rising. The irony is no comfort to Hollywood.

The accessibility of television has always made it an enemy of Hollywood, but two new factors are increasing its threat. One, bizarre though it may seem, is the manufacture by some of the major studios of films directly for television, films never intended for theatrical distribution at all, or only after many years following their presentation on TV. While Hollywood receives a welcome revenue from selling such films, the fact that they are not distributed in neighborhood theaters obviously excludes the box-office as a source of additional compensation. Thus, although the studios receive immediate cash, they lose the much wider market offered by the thousands of theaters throughout America. It is indeed strange to watch Hollywood actively engaged in aiding its most formidable competitor to obtain a product which that competitor then shows to its patrons—who might have been paying movie-goers—for nothing. More people than ever before are seeing Hollywood films, but most of them are not paying Hollywood for the privilege. That this policy is short-sighted is of course evident, but Hollywood is desperate, and the practice is becoming more prevalent among Hollywood studios every day.

Pictures made originally for movie-house distribution now appear on television within two years or even less of their initial appearance at theaters. The showing of almost-new films on television is often because they have failed at the box-office, compounded by the studios' pressing need for cash. Not too many years ago the selling of such films by major studios was limited to pictures which had been manufactured ten, fifteen, or even twenty years before, but times and conditions have changed.

Well, isn't Hollywood paid thumping sums for these films? The answer was once yes, but no longer. What was formerly a river of gold is drying up at the source. In its early stages, frantic for programs, television offered colossal sums for the right to show films. Since most of these pictures had outlived their pecuniary usefulness on theater screens, Hollywood rushed its old wares to this new market place. Whole libraries of films, representing decades of production, were sold. That was years ago. The storage vaults of major studios, once repositories of hundreds of films, have been stripped. The networks alone were consuming almost 400 films a year in the early seventies, including reruns; meanwhile, Hollywood's production is consistently decreasing. The purchase of Hollywood films by television continues, but it provides only a modest source of income, even when films sold shortly after their manufacture are included. Smash-hit pictures still get very high prices, but there are not many. Hollywood has almost nothing left to sell to television. An empty film vault is hardly an asset. Moreover, it is an elementary business principle that no industry can or should depend for its success or solvency on revenue from by-products. It must be sustained by its own primary product, in this case motion pictures for presentation in theaters.

Even when Hollywood films *are* sold to television, they are no longer pure profit. An aggregate of 12.4 percent of the sales prices of films to television is now being granted to writers, directors, actors, and other employees on all films completed after 1960, a payment formula that is steadily edging higher.

A second threat to Hollywood from the television companies is their decision to manufacture their own feature films in open competition with the major studios. By using their own studios and their own facilities, TV companies can make their pictures at a relatively low cost when compared to Hollywood studio charges for comparable productions. Television-trained personnel use shorter shooting schedules and are less meticulous. Television viewers are not overly discriminating; lack of quality is irrelevant to most non-paying customers. A considerable number of such films are being made by CBS and ABC which have created theatrical film-making arms for this purpose, and NBC is exploring the possibility of doing the same. Thus, television companies are in the interesting position of being supplier and consumer simultaneously. So fearful are the portents and the realities of this situation that a civil suit was instituted in 1970 against CBS and ABC by various major studios (Twentieth Century Fox abstained because it releases the feature films of these two companies in foreign territories), claiming a conspiratorial monopoly used to private advantage in violation of the Sherman and Clayton anti-trust acts.

Competition from European movie-makers is also having a negative impact. What was once a minor cult is now a fast-growing religion, particularly among the youth group which Hollywood is fighting to retain. The foreign-film followers comprise a sizeable and dedicated group of genuine cinéasts who espouse adult, mature, sophisticated pictures, and their lack of interest in American films is conspicuous and disconcerting. Some years ago a short-lived patriotic device was employed to curb this disloyalty by affixing the slogan "Made In Hollywood" on films manufactured in the United States. At best this was a hollow gesture, and if anything it made it easier for those movie-goers already eager to eschew Hollywood productions.

On top of all this, the New Hollywood is hurt by the censorship rulings embodied in the November 1968 Code of Self-Regulation of the Motion Picture Association of America as well as its subsequent revisions. Hollywood was smugly self-congratulatory at recognizing and even anticipating the new public morality, at the same time deftly avoiding the ever-present menace of repressive action from government. By replacing its antiquated censorship strictures with the more permissive rating system, the studios assumed that they had effectively protected themselves against all opposition. On the contrary, the more tolerant Code is being condemned on all sides. From every state in the union with the exception of Alaska (not yet heard from), there are a mounting number of bills pending in the legislatures aimed at curbing the "flagrant immorality" available on our screens.

Without question deliberate, arbitrary, unmitigated violence and offensively flagrant sexuality are being offered to audiences, and a quantitatively significant portion of that audience is beginning to object. The difference between liberty and license is hard to distinguish. Excessive violence and sex are now integral parts of many movies. How long this will continue in view of the intensifying dissent is a question. The threshold of tolerance may have been reached. So violent and vociferous has been the outcry that one is reminded of Hollywood in the 1930s when the Code was first hastily conceived to answer the fulminations against "vile and unwholesome" matter on the screen.

Criticism of the censorhip Code stems from the die-hard Puritans who would prefer inflexible moral restrictions and from civil libertarians who want no censorship at all. Hollywood is caught in the middle, nor has it even profited unduly from these pornographic shock-and-violence pictures, since most audiences soon find them unimaginative and unentertaining.

Thus we have Hollywood in the beginning of the seventies, thrashing about for solutions to its problems. And at this moment it faces the greatest crisis of all: the loss of the right to direct its own destiny, the ceding of its sovereignty to the multi-faceted giant conglomerates which have had no direct experience or knowledge of the film world.

Certainly the record of the conglomerates to date is not encouraging. Paramount, purchased by Gulf and Western, whose basic activities include metals, chemicals, and electrical products, has seen its entire West Coast executive staff removed from their Hollywood studio headquarters to a suite of offices in Beverly Hills in order to save money and permit the rental of these former studio offices as well as the studio stages to outsiders. Paramount has discharged hundreds of its employees and has been the subject of numerous For-Sale rumors. The first major action of Kinney National Services, which added Warner Brothers to its portfolio of parking lots, modular homes, and mortuaries, was to drastically slash the number of employees, to rent out as much studio space as possible, and to announce that only 25 percent of its own films would be shot in Hollywood. In addition, it moved most of the Warner Brothers New York executives and department heads to the Hollywood offices. Metro Goldwyn Mayer, which once dominated the industry, was purchased in 1969 by Kirk Kerkorian, a real estate magnate and resort hotel owner. Since then, it has seen its personnel decimated, its fabulous collection of furniture and costumes auctioned off, its English studio sold, its payroll trimmed by 35 percent, its New York offices moved to the West Coast, and three-quarters of its local real estate put on the sales block. Twentieth Century Fox fought off the financial courtship of the Walter Heller International Corporation, as well as that of the Broadway producer David Merrick, and barely emerged victor from a bitter proxy fight in August 1971 for studio control. It discharged its president, Richard Zanuck; divested Darryl Zanuck, Chairman of the Board, of much of his power; and has suffered mountainous losses which could easily lead to its purchase by another film-hungry conglomerate. To survive at all, Fox sold all its theaters in South Africa, discharged hundreds of its employees, and like Metro Goldwyn Mayer auctioned off thousands of props and pieces of furniture from its studio warehouses. United Artists, now part of the vast enterprises of Transamerica, Inc., whose principal interests are insurance and real estate, had its first major loss in many years in 1970, and it too has seen its personnel sharply reduced to lower the cost of overhead operations. In 1969 Columbia was almost engulfed by the Swiss Banque de Paris et des Pays-Bas, but it managed to stay independent. Universal is still an active candidate for merger, though Westinghouse and then Firestone failed to add it to their corporate portfolios. Among those film companies not ranked as major organizations, Embassy Films is a subsidiary of Avco Corporation, and the message of the future for the whole industry is writ large for all to see.

The full effect of the conglomerates on the film industry is as yet undetermined. We do know, and Richard Dyer Mac-Cann's *Hollywood In Transition* is instructive on this question, that faceless, impersonal, remote powers now dominate a historically individualistic industry. Are their decisions for the companies they own, the productions they approve, to be based on the concepts of film-makers or of businessmen? Are the interests of the parent companies likely to influence their choice of stories and subject matter? Are the conglomerates going to act as gigantic lobbies which either suppress or encourage special interests? Will they tolerate film subjects that might prove embarrassing or even inimical to one or more of the many other financial enterprises of the conglomerate? Possibly the most important query of all is whether the entry of these Big Business Goliaths may not prove to be the direct or indirect means of taking control of communications from those who have heretofore been the communicators—the writers, the directors, and the producers. Do the conglomerates presage an implicit and perhaps explicit attack on the freedom of ideas and self-expression, merely because of a conflict of interests?

We do not have any answers yet. Thus far, the conglomerates have not demonstrated any keener sensitivity to the role of the film-maker as creative artist than their predecessors did. The restrictions and limitations enjoined by them are much the same as those enforced by the Old Hollywood;

they want "safe" and profitable ventures. The owners of New Hollywood are no more interested in films dealing with sociological and political investigations and reforms, or artistic experiments, than were the Old Hollywood autocrats. They, too, believe that "message pictures" belong to Western Union, to quote the old Hollywood wheeze. The political activist producer exists in the New Hollywood, but just as precariously as he always did, for although a number of Hollywood's citizens as individuals are alert to civic, national, and international affairs, the Hollywood hierarchy which sponsors and distributes pictures does not like films that take or demand a political stand. Pictures dealing with "dynamite" themes, as both Old and New Hollywood call them, will still be memorable because there are so few.

However, the conglomerates are trying to effect one major change. They believe that the film industry should be supervised in much the same manner as any other business, and they are determined to use the same methods they employ in conducting their other commercial ventures, not recognizing that the film industry is a "sport" in the business world. In short, they are trying to industrialize an art.

Every large business has problems of labor and management, construction and merchandising, costs and prices, fluctuations in markets, competition from rivals; but the film industry is unique for at least two reasons. The first is that although it caters to a mass market, its products cannot be mass produced; each film bears little or no relationship to other films. The second is that is it the only industry of any magnitude which is basically and fundamentally an art and is dependent on the collaborative efforts of temperamental artists. It cannot be mechanized. In a bizarre fashion, it almost defies efficiency for its success, something the conglomerates find it hard to comprehend.

In an interview with David Selznick, as reported in Daniel Talbot's *Film: An Anthology*, Selznick observed:

"Hollywood might have become the center of a new human expression if it hadn't been grabbed by a little group of book-keepers." Mr. Selznick said this in a pre-conglomerate era; but it is even more applicable today when the "little group of book-keepers" has been replaced by a large group of business and efficiency experts whose interests are not basically humanistic.

The film industry cannot be treated like any other business. It is and always will be a highly fluid enterprise that demands constant attention as well as a tolerant understanding of its creative inconsistencies. Certainly it is not a business that can be conducted long-distance. To try to exercise leadership and responsibility from New York, the home turf of the conglomerates, is courting disaster. Hollywood is a breeding ground for hourly crises and emergencies that demand immediate decisions; film-makers are not distinguished for their logic or their emotional stability. As Gilbert Seldes remarked, they have a high "potential capacity for disaster," and to avoid it requires continuous and sympathetic supervision. At least the film tycoons of the Old Hollywood—tyrannical, despotic, crude, domineering, even corrupt—had one virtue: they were passionately and unswervingly devoted to the one business they knew, the making of films.

The majority of the conglomerates, conservative in their thinking, will simply not take the chances that these former industry leaders accepted as routine. The conglomerate executives see films as an orderly way to make money; but film-making is not orderly; it defies order and what is even more inimical to the conglomerate philosophy, it requires and demands constant risk-taking. "You've got to gamble," Richard Zanuck said of films, "The movie industry isn't a slide rule business and never will be. It's still the world's biggest crap game." It is this "world's biggest crap game" that the conglomerates have joined, and few members of the new clan are gamblers.

The studio heads who dominated the Old Hollywood were no less profit conscious than the men controlling it today. In their own way they too were trying to make factory-fashioned products, and the conventional, stereotyped "family films" that emerged from Hollywood during their reign were often as shoddy and vacuous as any films being distributed today. But they also sponsored and produced a number of distinguished films, films originating largely in the 1930s and 1940s, which have become authentic demonstrations of the film as an art form, films which have been revived again and again, films which exacted tributes at the time of their initial appearance and are still eagerly sought by discriminating viewers whenever they are shown. These men gambled occasionally on films that did not follow "safe," routine patterns, sponsored projects that were not arbitrarily designed for mediocre minds and mass audiences.

Hollywood's Golden Period was no accident of economic climate or luck; it was the product of a handful of men who put all their energies and native shrewdness into making Hollywood a by-word for success in the entertainment world. Yes, a writer-director said of them, they were "monsters and pirates and bastards right to the bottom of their feet, but they *loved* movies, and they protected the people who worked for them. Some of the jerks running the business now don't even have faces."

If the Hollywood pioneers were sometimes contemptuous of the artists they hired, a contempt stemming from ignorance, they were also respectful of talent. They knew and appreciated the mass-mind, for they *were* the mass-mind, and they ran their organizations with absolute, but successful, despotism. If nothing else, they were showmen, which the fiducial, methodical conglomerate executives are not.

Conglomerates are necessarily more concerned with profit than even the greediest of the film kings of the past.

Their corporate structure makes this inevitable; they have a responsibility and an obligation to their thousands of stockholders. They cannot afford to sponsor anything that does not appeal to the largest number of people, and this virtually eliminates art, which tends to attract only the discriminating.

Consequently, though much has been written and spoken about the New Freedom in the New Hollywood, the liberation of the artist as an individual, the encouragement of the young film-makers, and the advent of personal autonomy, the reality is quite different. The conglomerates want profitable results as swiftly as possible or they will abandon motion pictures completely. Should the film arm of their gigantic nexus of enterprises become infected with the virus of failure, amputation via divestiture will be the recommended cure, lest that arm poison the rest of the corporate body. In years gone by, the theory that "there's nothing wrong with the picture business that a good picture can't cure," as enunciated by Nicholas Schenck, then president of Metro Goldwyn Mayer, was believed by the Hollywood fraternity and often proved correct. But in these days of shifting audience values, even if the word "good" is defined as Schenck intended it, that is, profitable, there is no longer any formula that can help the industry make "good" (profitable) pictures.

Will Hollywood become a ghost town? Probably not, but it will survive largely as a museum of vanished glories. It will never regain the prestige or worldwide acceptance it had unless drastic changes are effected in its basic structure. Nevertheless, Hollywood continues to make films. Agents, writers, directors, actors, and producers still work, despite the grim statistics and the difficulties that have been described. It is to their roles in a world David Selznick described as a land "full of crumbling pyramids" that we now turn.

THE AGENT

*An agent is a guy who is sore because the actor gets 90%
of what he makes.*

ALVA JOHNSTON

Hollywood is bounded on the north, south, east, and west by
agents. They may be revered or reviled, extolled or ex-
ecrated, but they cannot be ignored. Text books on film often
advise the student that there are six essential elements required for the making of a motion picture: the producer, the
writer, the director, the cast, the cameraman, and the editor.
They are making a colossal mistake (Hollywood rarely
makes any other kind!) in omitting the agent, for none of
these six components of picture-making could function without him.

Although written over twenty-five years ago, Leo Rosten's definition of an agent in his *Hollywood: The Movie
Colony—The Movie Makers* is still accurate:

> *In Hollywood nothing is certain but death, and taxes and
> agents. Agents, like producers, are the sacrificial goats of*

the movie colony, which confuses their personalities with their functions. They are the salesmen and professional representatives of actors, writers, directors. They sell talent and stories; they get their clients jobs, contracts, raises, or concessions. They guard prestige and bargaining power. They are experts in marketing anything from a pair of legs to an unwritten synopsis. Agents get ten per cent of the salary of their clients, by whom they are generally resented, and haggle, plead, coax, fight with producers, by whom they are generally disliked.

Any evaluation of Hollywood agents must first acknowledge their incontestable power in the industry, a power that has grown over the years. The contemporary agent—or "artist's representative" as he prefers to be called—is a vital part of the entire Hollywood mechanism. He still operates as a merchandiser of wares, selling writers, actors, directors, designers, musicians, as well as literary material for the screen. He has, however, transcended the role of mere salesman. The expansion of his jurisdiction and authority has come about not so much through desire or purposeful activity on the part of the agent himself, but, oddly enough, through the relinquishing of power by his customers, the studios.

There was a time when the studios had almost total, if not despotic, control over the numerous artists and craftsmen needed for the making of films. Those were the days when anyone who showed talent (and many who did not) were granted employment contracts binding them for as long as seven years to an individual studio for which they worked on an exclusive basis. This was in the 1940s and 1950s, Before Conglomerates, when each studio was run by a single man, the legendary Hollywood tycoon. Each studio had hundreds of employees in its stable—writers, directors, actors, producers, designers, musicians, technicians—all subject to the whim of the Front Office. In that period the agent served the practical purpose of selling his client to a studio, and drew his weekly commission for having done so, but there his services and influence ended.

The feudal chiefs and their prerogatives are no more. No studio has a retinue of vassals eager to do its bidding. Today no studio offers long- or even short-term contracts if they can be avoided; no studio has the luxury of being able to select players, writers, directors from its own stable. There is no stable, yet films must be made. Hence, the agent and *his* stable have come to the fore. The servant has become the master. It is now the agent who controls the talent without which movies cannot be made. Needless to add, this reversal of authority is bitterly resented by the studios, but they have no choice. They willingly assisted in the dissolution of their empires, leaving the agent, via his clients, the single most powerful factor in Hollywood. Although several major studios are encountering severe economic problems involving serious discussion of re-financing and re-organization, not a single important Hollywood agency has closed its doors during this period of crisis in the industry.

Though Hollywood itself is no longer a major film center, the Hollywood agent's prominence is evident wherever and whenever a potential film-maker conceives of a project and says to himself or his associates, "Now let's see, can we get——, and who handles him?" "Who handles him?" are the key words, for at that moment the agent becomes the most significant contributor to the proposed film, and without him the chances of its ever becoming a completed picture are almost non-existent.

The agent is so taken for granted in the film industry that few people have examined his role and function. What is an agent? What does he do?

To "private people," the pitying term employed by the

film industry for those not connected with motion pictures, it would appear that an agent is no more than a go-between whose sole function is to find a job for someone. On that assumption, his operation seems very like that of an ordinary employment agency. However, an agent in Hollywood is much more than the middleman who negotiates the employment terms, consummates the deal, and goes his way.

In the world of "private people," once an employment agent has procured a position for his client and collected the fee, he may never see the client again. In Hollywood the relationship between client and agent may persist for years, starting with the initial quest for a job and continuing on long after its termination. This is because a client seeking a job in films is unlike any other client in any other industry.

In the pretentious, theatrical, flamboyant ambience that gives Hollywood its identity, those who work there experience extraordinary demands and desires. A film agent is confronted daily, sometimes hourly, by calculated eccentricities, obsessions, compulsions, vanities, hysterical extravagances, mercurial jealousies, and passionate idiosyncrasies. That ninety percent of these are arrant self-indulgence does not make the agent's task easier. But he is not representing "private people"; he is involved exclusively with "artists," actual or self-styled, and the personality problems that a Hollywood artist presents are as complex as they are bizarre.

Hollywood is an in-group in spite of its thirty thousand or more employees. It is a world of and to itself. The man who works on the creative level in Hollywood is convinced that he is different in kind as well as degree from any other employee in any other enterprise. He is an artist. He is certain that this gives him special privileges and prerogatives. The megalomania of actors, especially of stars, has been highly publicized, but it is equally true of directors, writers, producers, cameramen, art designers, costumers, make-up experts, animators, drama coaches, musicians, dancers, composers, lyricists, and singers.

Every contract ever written has the word "artist" splashed through dozens of paragraphs; the unions and guilds invariably refer to their members as artists. It is an accepted and approved classification. And the artists, real or spurious, have adopted the classic pose of the man of talent who is remote and detached from the mundane world of commercialism. Their assumed disinterest in such crass matters as compensation has demanded of the film agent a shrewd business ability combined with a considerable knowledge of primitive psychology. The agent must choreograph his movements carefully; he must cater to his client's seeming disregard for the boring intricacies of the contract, at the same time making sure that the artist is protected down to the last minute detail in order to avoid later repercussions. This is not simple, since the artist is never present during the negotiations. The agent, however, is thoroughly aware that once the terms have been "finalized" or "concretized" or "firmed" or "locked-up" (four Hollywood solecisms), the artist will probably show himself as hard-headed and cunning as any agent. Since it is considered important to maintain the fiction of aloof indifference, no actor or writer or director would ever confront a prospective employer and openly discuss "the numbers," Hollywood's term for salary. In a philosophic sense, the refusal to participate in conversations about money dramatizes the schism so evident in the whole world of films, the conflict between art and industry. This dichotomy does not trouble the agent. He has no illusion to perpetuate; he is not an artist, real or counterfeit. His only talent, and not one to be slighted, is his ability to make money for his client and thus for himself.

One of the most important words affecting the uneasy liaison between a client and his agent does not appear in any contract although it is common currency in every Hollywood office. The word is "happy." When a client is not "happy" during an engagement, buzzers sound in executive suites, documents are re-examined in legal departments, and agents are hastily summoned. For the "unhappy" actor or writer or director suddenly finds himself literally unable to act or write or direct with his usual skill and authority—until he is "happy" again. Since the skill in each instance cannot be summarily replaced, and since millions of dollars hinge on good performances, this matter becomes a crisis that requires the expert therapeutic treatment of the "unhappy" artist's agent. The conference that ensues is invariably solved by the curing or removal of the "offense" which made the artist "unhappy." The source of the artist's unhappiness may be a secondary member of the cast with whom the artist is feuding, the need for a chauffeur-driven car for transportation to the studio, a desire for the remodeling and redecoration of a dressing room, or some other item that was not in the formal agreement the artist signed when he was "happy." It is the agent's task to redress this delicate imbalance, to be the moderator and pacifier. He has to solve the problem without antagonizing the studio employer (necessary for future business) and at the same time maintain the confidence of his client (present income provider). This requires a superior negotiating facility because the agent knows that if the client is not made "happy," he will accuse the agent of ineptitude, if not downright disloyalty. And the agent who does not keep his client "happy" will soon lose him to another agent.

The agent who pretends to any degree of competence in his highly competitive, nerve-wracking trade must not merely demonstrate diplomacy and acumen in business. He must also devote a sizeable portion of his time to keeping his client "happy" on matters that have nothing to do with the making of films. An agent must be all things to all clients.

One of an agent's many roles may be that of efficient, and discreet, Cupid. This assignment can become especially delicate when the artist's current love is not his wife. Thus the agent is involved in ensuring secrecy, in arranging rendezvous, and at the same time in protecting the artist from an exposure which might destroy his marriage and, even more significant to the agent, his career. The agent is, in addition, a marriage counsellor, a calling he often carries on while abetting an extramarital affair. This calls for logistics of a superior nature. His unwritten duties may involve him in providing bail for a client, lending him money during workless periods, sending gifts or congratulatory telegrams in his name on appropriate social or business occasions (they are indistinguishable in Hollywood), and protecting him against an unfriendly or antagonistic press. Beyond these activities, agents are also expected to run errands: they rent or buy homes for their clients, shop for them, arrange hotel and travel accommodations, theater tickets, and restaurants (the "right" table is of incalculable significance), and they are always available as escorts or companions at gala affairs or parties. One agent has achieved distinction by lending his female clients a mink coat for all important social (business) occasions. To buttress a client's ego, cater to his neuroses, and allay his depressions, the agent is also on call as an amateur psychiatrist.

Although the only source of remuneration for a Hollywood agent is the sale of a client's services or his literary material, he must also be prepared to offer authoritative tax advice—counsel which must be on international as well as national matters. This need, of course, has been occasioned by the growing number of artists who prefer to reside outside the United States for tax-shelter reasons (though these are not the reasons advanced by their publicity agents). In consequence, any agent worth his ten percent commission has a retinue of highly trained aides and consultants who work with him—not only tax experts but accountants, business managers, personal administrators, and attorneys. Certain agents maintain an affiliation with an investment counselor, since the span of a Hollywood career (the exceptions are few) is rarely over ten years, particularly in the case of performers.

Apart from his values as a salesman, business guardian, and confidant, the next most substantial asset a Hollywood agent can provide his client is information. All agencies have "leg men" who haunt studios, restaurants, race tracks, theater opening nights, dinner parties, film premieres, any and all places where film folk assemble and fraternize. The leg man's sole purpose is to pick up information. What picture is being considered? Is the property available for sale? Can the agent secure its representation or does a rival agent already control it? Does the projected film need a writer, a director, a cameraman, a composer, a designer? Is a certain player or writer "unhappy" with his current agent? Facts, rumors, whispers, confidences, intimations, all carefully recorded in a little black book and all presented meticulously at agency staff meetings—ordinarily twice a week at eight in the morning. Nor is this gossip gathering and its dissemination without worth. It is only by such checking and questioning that the agent can serve his client well, for the client cannot find out on his own all the various maneuvers going on in Hollywood on any single day, which pieced together may mean a job or a sale for him.

With the disappearance of the long-term contract which permitted an agent to rest comfortably for years on his commission, the contemporary agent is faced with the unpleasant necessity of securing a series of jobs for his clients. Few people in Hollywood any longer have continuous employment at a single studio. They shuttle from one job to another and are more often "at liberty" than on a company payroll. Even stars have to accept one-picture agreements, or in more fortunate circumstances a multiple-picture pact (usually limited to three films), while deals for directors are generally confined to a single picture. With the exception of stars and directors, the prevalent assignment in today's film world consists of a week-to-week deal with no guaranteed period of compensation or, at best, a very limited number of weeks. Thus an agent has a stable of clients who repeatedly face the prospect of being discharged after relatively short terms of employment. And to find employment for them he must work harder and longer than he ever did before to keep his clients on salary.

Every agent has a sword of Damocles over his head—the legal right of the client to terminate his agreement with the agent if ninety days should elapse during which the agent does not present a job proposal "with compensation equal to his past customary theatrical motion picture salary for fifteen days employment." There is a further escape clause for the actor-client which on close examination seems more caressive of his vanity than anything else. The agent must bring him an offer from an employer "at a salary commensurate with the actor's prestige." How calculable prestige is remains baffling, but in ego-conscious Hollywood such jabberwocky is not unusual, especially in legal documents.

It must be obvious by now that the work habits of a Hollywood agent would have to be unconventional. As angry clients have complained for years, the agent is almost never in his office. Since his job is to ferret out or invent demands for the services of his clients, he is constantly traveling from studio to studio, buttonholing producers and executives, gossiping with players and writers on his quest for film tips of any kind. He sees his client either at breakfast conferences—7:30 A.M. is not an unusual time—or after 7:30 P.M. in his office, or later at his client's home. Because production is now worldwide, his sleep is interrupted by phone calls at odd hours from all over. Since New York is vital to his business, and there is a time differential between the East and West coasts, he frequently gets up at five or six to consult with his eastern associates. Agencies of any size have a direct telephone connection between their Hollywood and their New York branches, and the bills are astronomical. One well-known agent makes frequent trips to New York to phone the studio heads in Hollywood, since he knows they will always accept long distance calls in preference to local ones.

The agent is always present at "sneak," meaning unannounced and unpublicized film previews, as well as at public premieres of any picture involving his clients, and he is an essential and protective (for his clients) part of the "sidewalk conferences" that follow such showings. His leisure time is his business time and vice versa; he makes no distinctions between them. If an important client or an important prospective buyer enjoys racing, gambling, skiing, tennis, golf, cards, swimming, scuba diving, or Scrabble, the smiling agent is there as a participant or attendant. Most agents eschew liquor since luncheons and dinners as well as breakfasts involve convivial imbibing, and an agent must keep a clear head. Dining in general is a problem, for an agent rarely eats at home; therefore masseurs and health clubs (where clients and producers can be seen at the same time) are a part of an agent's health regimen. He is always on the move; he is almost never alone; "to contact" people is his way of life.

Special notice should be taken of an odd use to which the telephone is put in the service of jobless clients. The Hollywood artist who is unemployed, and therefore not paying commissions, finds it very hard to make an appointment with his agent and even harder to reach him on the telephone. No agent likes to spend time with an impecunious client unless there is a position in the offing for him. Still, agents are human, all rumors to the contrary, and they dislike telling clients that the job situation is bleak. So they instruct their secretaries to return the client's beseeching phone calls at a time when the client will probably not be there and to leave a message that the agent has called. The lunch period is most satisfactory for this. This ploy is known in Hollywood as making a "credit call," since the agent gets credit for having telephoned. Hardly an example of moral rectitude, such a ruse is part of an agent's working day.

It is no longer possible for just anyone to become an agent, although the wry comment of Milton Pickman, one of Hollywood's most successful practitioners of the craft, is still relevant: "Not every guy can walk in off the street and be an agent—but *almost* any guy can." At least the "guy" is now required to abide by many more standards, regulations, and proscriptions than prevailed in the days when his entire equipment consisted of a scratch pad and a pencil, and his office was any convenient telephone booth. The majority of today's agents belong to a mutual protective association called The Artists Manager's Guild, which has over one hundred members. There is even an Agency Code of Fair Practice. All accredited agents—and there can be no other kind—are under the jurisdiction and supervision of the California State Labor Code. Before a would-be agent can begin to take "ten percent off the top," he must first submit a formal application and fill out a rather complicated questionnaire attesting to his financial stability, character, and background. In addition, his application for a license to practice the art of agentry must be accompanied by two affidavits from "reputable residents" which assert and confirm that he "is a person of good moral character." There is a filing fee of $25, an additional $100 for the license itself, and the payment of $50 for each branch office in the state of California. Supplementing these assessments is a surety bond in the form of a deposit of $1000 with the Labor Commissioner of the State of California. Once his license is granted, the agent cannot transfer it to anyone else and it must be renewed annuallly. To defeat the telephone booth locale, the agent must maintain a satisfactory office or place where his business is conducted. This provision reads, ". . . failure of the artist's manager or agency to maintain a regular office for the transaction of business for a period of three consecutive months shall be cause for cancellation or termination of the contract." Nor can the agent move his office without written consent from the Labor Commissioner.

An odd and unexpected clause in the California State Code of Labor concerning agents has the following stipulation: "No artist's manager shall give any false information or make any false promises or representations concerning an engagement or employment to any applicant who applies for an engagement or employment." To apply this exquisitely ethical injunction to any salesman is wry enough; to exact it from a Hollywood agent whose clients are actual or pretended artists would be economical suicide for him. To put it bluntly, any agent who followed this injunction with even partial fidelity would invite catastrophe. To be diplomatic, to be persuasive, to dissemble, to disavow, to cajole, to flatter, to distort, to change, to pretend, to conceal, to mislead, to compromise—some or all of these practices are the agent's stock-in-trade.

Even if the agent were the soul of sincerity, it would be impossible for him to report the negative comments he hears from prospective employers about his clients. Can he tell his actor-client—and keep him "happy"—that a major executive said of him: "He can't act his way out of a paper hat." Or of a director: "He can't direct traffic." Or of a writer: "He couldn't write his name with an X." Or of a cameraman: "He couldn't handle a Brownie 2A." Or of an art-designer: "He couldn't design a jock-strap"—all typical Hollywood witticisms. Nor does the artist want to hear them. All the artist wants to know is the size of the salary, when the engagement starts, how long is the guarantee, what size his billing will be. Nothing else matters and the agent knows it. An agent who does not make any "false promises" or give any "false information" to his client while endeavoring to snare a job for him is an anomaly. The agent who claims that he is abiding by the maxim Thou Shalt Not Lie is lying—or bankrupt.

All these regulatory measures installed by the State of California came into being because of flagrant corruption and abuse by Hollywood's first agents in the days when many agencies included a "talent school." Under this guise innocents lured by the promise of instant fame and riches were mercilessly gulled and defrauded. This condition no longer prevails, and though agents may not be loved or approved of or even respected, their position in Hollywood today is impregnable. There would be no Hollywood without them.

Most agencies, small or large, divide their activities into two spheres: the selling of literary material, known as properties, and the marketing of personal services, known as flesh peddling. The latter heading includes selling the talents and abilities of actors, writers, directors, cameramen, producers, lyricists, technicians, and so on. All have varying values (commissions) to an agent, but the ones demanding the greatest concentration are, of course, the actors, for an actor's remuneration, when he is successful, far exceeds that of any other client the agent "handles." Furthermore, the representation of a name-actor or star is an important advertisement for the agency and acts as an inducement for other potential clients to affiliate with that agency. There is always the fantasy-wish on the part of lesser-known actors that the agent may accomplish the same miracle for them. In addition, a star invariably has an entourage of favorite subordinates with whom he prefers to work, such as secondary players, directors, make-up men, cameramen, musicians, lighting technicians. Thus the star's agent is able to become the representative of other people who are commissionable, and who might not otherwise get jobs or who would normally hire some other agent.

Catering to a star is not easy, for a star is just as aware of his or her value to an agent as the agent is. As a result, stars are invariably represented by a single executive within the agency who is uniquely responsible for everything involving that actor, starting with his "deal," and including his selection of scripts, directors, producers, cameramen, and so forth. It is not inconceivable for such an agent to devote his entire time to one actor, who will make no move without this agent's sanction. The agent assigned to a star automatically becomes a "star" himself within the agency, since he alone is responsible for the enormous commissions accruing from the actor and his satellites. Assuming the actor-agent relationship to be durable, and even in quixotic Hollywood such alliances have persisted for many years, this fortunate agent often becomes a very rich man. In fact, owing to the improvidence of actors and their passion for conspicuous consumption, it is often the agent who ends his career in affluence, whereas the actor may end his days as a beneficiary of the Motion Picture Relief Fund.

The care-and-feeding of actors is time-consuming and sometimes unrewarding for the agent. The agent who unearths an actor whom he believes to have great, though still unrecognized, talent must possess both infinite faith and patience. There are agents in Hollywood who "carry" such an actor for years, only to see him fail in the end, or—the most bitter irony of all—succeed and be lured away by a larger agency. The grooming of an unknown actor can be a relentless and painstaking process for the conscientious agent. To prevent a summary rejection by the studio, the agent must make certain that the screen test projects his client's best points, and that he is "seen" on the most important social occasions. Then the agent must be sure that the studio gives the actor appropriate roles once he is accepted, that his contract is not inequitable, and, of course, that he stays "happy." Although the better equipped and better staffed agencies would seem to be the ones who could indulge in this costly, often discouraging, training process, that is not the case. This tedious nurturing is usually taken on by the small agents who are actuated by hope, even though they may ultimately lose the client they have so carefully prepared. In any event, many a Hollywood star owes his current success and fame to an agent whose loyalty and steadfast devotion sustained and supported him through years of obscurity.

Next to actors in importance (that is, commission potential) are the directors and the writers, who also come in for considerable attention by the industrious agents. Of the two, the director is of greater concern, especially today when he has taken on box-office allure. Film afficionados follow the careers of directors with greater interest and fidelity than they do those of stars, and while film buffs are not the bulk of the American audience, they are growing in number. The box-office magnetism of the director, like that of the star, is of calculable money value to the astute agent not only for the director's own salary, but as a way of attracting new clients. A number of celebrated directors have what is called a stock company of players, assistant directors, grips, and so on, with whom they work amiably and efficiently; and this group of loyal affiliates also contributes to the agent's coffers. The film director as such will be discussed later, but from the viewpoint of the agent, the director is fast becoming an expanding source of revenue. Screenwriters are a class by themselves; very few attain the enormous salaries accorded stars and directors and producers; nevertheless, they represent a sizeable portion of an agent's total commissions, and a number of smaller agents specialize in vending their talents. High-salaried producers also represent valuable commission sources as they too like to surround themselves with faithful subordinates, and once again the agent is the ten percent beneficiary. Thus it goes on down the salary scale of merchandise offered by the agent—cameramen, art designers, composers, lyricists, technicians—all grist to the agent's money mill.

Mention should be made of executives, who are occasionally represented by agents, but who pay no commission. This is not an index of altruism or friendship. It is patent that a highly placed executive can be of enormous value to an agent on both the recommendatory and the negotiation levels, and the agent is much too astute to exact a commission from a man who can be of significant assistance in a hundred different ways during a year. The executive-agent relationship is a shining example of *quid pro quo*, and such special clients are known as non-commissionable clients.

When we turn from actors, directors, writers, and producers to the more prosaic but highly profitable marketing of literary properties—books, plays, stories—we enter an entirely different world of salesmanship. A number of agents prefer this to the handling of human merchandise. "Books don't talk," as one of them explained.

The methods used by Hollywood agents to market manuscripts or literary properties are in direct contrast to those used by East Coast agents. Among New York's literary representatives the ethics governing the submission of manuscripts have been unchanged for many years. Generally, a manuscript is submitted to one publisher at a time, which accounts for the numerous stories of individual books that failed to achieve publication until dozens of rejections had been accumulated. Not so in Hollywood. Simultaneous submission is the rule and the practice. Even before the invention of xerography, Hollywood agents had copies of a literary work reproduced by mimeograph and sent to as many potential buyers as possible. Whereas formerly the number of such submissions was limited to the major studios, this is no longer true in the era of the independent producer who has no permanent studio affiliation. As many as a hundred or more copies of an individual manuscript may be submitted from an agent's office. The bill for this spate of reproductions, incidentally, is paid by the client whether he approves or not, and whether the manuscript is sold or not.

Another difference between the East Coast literary agent and his Hollywood counterpart is that a New York agent is generally well read, discriminating about literature, and therefore capable of suggesting useful revisions to writers. For the Hollywood agent to offer editorial advice to a writer-client would be odd, for the agent is concerned solely with narrative and production values. Will it suit a certain star? Is it economically feasible? Is the subject matter attractive? Will it have a mass appeal? Will it satisfy foreign audiences? Is it too controversial? These and many more questions of a strictly commercial nature are the agent's only concerns, and none of them has to do with qualitative literary judgments about style, structure, or language. Strange as it may seem, even these commercial questions are rarely given *serious* consideration by the Hollywood agent, for they are all answered by the studio's response to the single question: Will it sell? By virtue of considerable experience he has learned that any opinion, impression, or idea he might have about improving or changing a story is probably pointless; stories he might have considered unfilmable (unsaleable) have often caught the fancy of a producer and been purchased. Why correct or amend a story when there are no accepted guidelines? Producer taste and selectivity are impossible to predict. The agent's credo is, therefore, let the buyer decide.

There are some agents who offer critical "literary" guidance to clients, but they are few. Nor does the writer-client resent his agent's lack of editorial advice. He wants an opinion from his agent, but not on whether the written work is outstanding; he wants to know whether it will sell. He and the agent are as one on this. The writer who accepts editorial assistance from his agent may even be imperilling his work, for the ordinary agent knows little or nothing about writing. If the manuscript sells, it is good; if it does not, it is bad. Hollywood agents act on this belief by (with rare exceptions) automatically submitting all written projects for sale.

There is a corollary to this indiscriminate submission of manuscripts. Invariably, as each copy of a multiple submission manuscript is forwarded, phone calls are made to selected recipients, each of whom is assured with absolute solemnity and engaging dishonesty that it is the "only copy" and that the receiver of the call is getting what is called a "first look." This charade has been going on for years, and for the same number of years prospective buyers have succumbed to the agent's bland lie. As a result of this "first look" fable, frenzied story analysts or readers employed by studios to synopsize literary submissions frequently work all night to profit from an alleged advantage over competitors who are not offered the "first look"—so desperate is the competition for story material. This custom originated long ago when there were fewer agents, and studios and executives had "favored" agents who catered to them; but what was once a courtesy is now a wholesale deception, and no one has had the courage to expose it for the fraud it is.

An adjunct to this absurd "first look" is the sending simultaneously of form telegrams to all those chosen to receive the manuscript, quoting the price of the film rights and requesting that bids be registered with the agent by a specified time, usually within twenty-four hours after the receipt of the agent's wire. This simply makes official the situation the prospective purchasers were in from the beginning—that is, competing with the simultaneous readings of other prospective purchasers.

Any discussion of literary submissions, editorial counsel by agents, or "first looks" brings up the question of how agents select their material in the first place. What is their screening process? How do they decide on what stories to market, since it is obvious that no agent can approve every manuscript that comes to his desk?

The most negligent and illiterate agent is aware of the contents of the material that he accepts for possible sale. To be "aware" does not necessarily mean he has read it. It would be unjust to state that agents never read what they are submitting, but it is simple truth to say that they do not always do so. An agent can make twenty phone calls and close three remunerative deals in the two to four hours he would spend reading a book-length manuscript or screenplay. Thus the synopsis system has evolved. A staff synopsizer will condense a manuscript to one or two or three pages so that the agent can be "aware of the contents." But not all agents can afford this luxury. Agents who lack readers and are unwilling or unable to read manuscripts themselves submit the *unread* material to a studio or studios on the "first look" basis, but with a proviso that in return for this "first look" the studio will give the agent a synopsis! Since all studios still have story departments, large or small, this reciprocity has become established practice. Once the agent has the studio synopsis, he can "discuss" the material with the writer, leaving the impression that he has read every word of it.

Having read the studio synopsis and made an affirmative decision to market the manuscript, the agent either slightly rewrites or otherwise disguises the studio version and subsequently sends it to other studios, together with the manuscript. On occasion he does not even trouble to include the manuscript, for he knows that like himself, the producer also prefers a short synopsis to a long book. It may well be asked whether *anyone*, other than the writer, the agency reader, or the studio reader, ever reads the full material. The answer is that many a story unread by the agent or the purchaser except in synopsis has been bought for hundreds of thousands of dollars. This mode of buying will be discussed later, but its oddity and the irresponsibility of all concerned are self-evident.

Why don't studios get their story material directly from authors? Because a number of plagiarism suits have been instituted against film studios by both amateur and professional writers. The agent does not offer absolute protection against such suits, but custom as well as practice has made it most unusual for an agent to be party to such legal action on behalf of a client. Studios or purchasers are relatively permanent, whereas clients are transient. Thus the studio and the agent cooperate with each other, the agent becoming what in studio parlance is an "accredited" source for literary material. Unsolicited, unaccredited material is returned unopened to the sender by the studio, together with a form letter recommending that the writer use an "accredited" representative, meaning an agent, if he wishes his manuscript to be considered.

The agent, therefore, plays two roles: he is of aid in

discouraging or averting possible plagiarism suits and—though this remains one of those inconsistent fantasies of Hollywood—he has supposedly read the material, assessed its value for films, and consequently given it a professional blessing before submitting it to the studio. The studio happily assumes someone versed in evaluating stories has passed judgment on it. This hallucination persists despite the studio's knowledge that the agent has probably only read a synopsis prepared by the studio itself. Literary life is not complex in Hollywood.

As of 1971, possibly the largest, most successful, most stable and respected agency in Hollywood was the William Morris Agency. Founded in 1898, it has a staff of five hundred and fifty employees and, in addition to its Hollywood home office, has branches in New York, Chicago, London, Paris, Rome, Madrid, and Munich. It has fifteen distinct departments on its Hollywood premises, owns and occupies its own building, and does an annual business volume of close to $12 million in commissions. Another large agency is CMA, or Creative Management Associates, which in 1970 had a gross billing of $122 million, and took in over $11 million in clients' commissions. This agency maintains offices throughout the world, and in addition to the cities where the William Morris Agency has branches, adds Tokyo, Sydney, Las Vegas, and Miami.

These two agencies are examples of the four or five giants that bestride Hollywood. There are numerous smaller firms, which share the spoils, but as the history of Hollywood has shown, they usually die away or are merged with the larger organizations. The monetary value of an agency resides exclusively, of course, in its roster of clients. Thus, when important (meaning high-salaried) clients emerge from a small agency, the large agency goes into immediate action. If the large agency cannot lure the client away from the small agency, it does the next best thing: it buys the small agency. The merger is ordinarily accompanied by the retention on a salary basis of the small agency's headman, so that the so-called loyalty of the desired client is not imperilled. Once the new clients have indicated satisfaction with their new, larger sponsor, the owner of the original agency may be invited to resign. When this happens, he is paid off and enjoined from entering the agency business for a number of agreed on years in order to prevent future competition. Occasionally the headman of a small agency is of such signal value that he stays with the large agency as an employee, even though his personal clientele may no longer use his services. In Hollywood as elsewhere in America, Big Business is impatient with Small Business.

We have mentioned the luring of clients away from small agencies by the large ones. This is a euphemism; "stealing" is a more accurate word, and despite its interdiction the vice is widespread. There is an established protocol in stealing clients from a rival establishment, a ritual mating-dance. The desired client is invited to elegant dinner parties to meet influential studio heads or executives; gifts are sent to him; his friendship is cultivated; gratuitous professional counsel is proferred—all leading to that critical moment when the client himself (the agent rarely if ever makes the first overt move) suggests that he transfer his allegiance from his own agent to the courting agent. Naturally, this strategy is only used when the client in question has attained a high-salary status. The low-salaried client does not pay enough commission to warrant such a courtship.

More often than not, the client is willing to be seduced. It is a matter of prestige. A large agency is a status symbol. The answer to "Who handles you?" is an index of importance and rank. There are fashions in agents, of course, and now and again the "in" agent is a small, hard-working, conscientious owner of a one-man office; but by and large, the distinction of being "on the list" of a major agency is avidly sought.

Another method of acquiring the clients of rival agents is the honorable course of actually purchasing the artist's contract from the small agent with the consent of the artist; when this is done, the small agent is compensated either by an outright sum or by a percentage of the artist's future income for a period of time.

Another technique is the split-fee procedure. When the desired client remains stubbornly loyal to his original representative, the large agent proposes that both agencies represent the artist and that all commissions be divided equally. This proposal is based on the theory (sometimes an actuality) that the large agent can be of greater assistance to the client, and eventually the small agent is forced to capitulate. The split-fee is basically a delaying, foot-in-the-door tactic, since ultimately the large agent begins to dominate and direct the career of the artist to such an extent that he willingly abandons his prior representative. The small agent, despite his ability, or in many cases, because of it, is continually subject to piratical forays.

One group of agents has escaped the octopean attention of the large agencies, mainly because its clientele is not numerically substantial nor are the commissions very lucrative. These are the specialized agencies. The film industry's appetite for talent ranges far beyond those artists represented by the majority of agents, and consequently an unusual category has sprung into being. This is composed of small organizations whose clients include stunt men, bit players (small parts), character actors, swordsmen, motorcyclists, freaks, circus performers, magicians, horsemen, special effects experts, ethnic players, divers, balloonists, jugglers, trained animals, sky jumpers, midgets, dwarfs, airplane pilots, skaters, and so on. There is always a "ten percenter" available to comply with any need, however bizarre it may seem.

Not content with their normal operations as salesmen of human and literary merchandise, agents have extended their power into two new domains. One is "packaging," a term borrowed from Madison Avenue, a relatively new phenomenon in the film industry; the other is the entry of the agent into the producer ranks. The two developments are definitely connected.

Packaging is simply the stitching together of two or three or more elements required for a film. These may include a star, a director, a book, and a writer; or a screenplay, a director, and a producer, thus making a tidy cinematic project. The advent of agency packaging has been cheered by the studios, which is a sign of their ineptitude or indolence, since in so doing the studios are demonstrating their inability to put together packages of their own. This abdication is welcomed by alert agents who find packaging extraordinarily lucrative: ten percent off the top of four salaries is better than ten percent off the top of one. In addition, since the contents of a package (producer, star, director, etc.) are controlled by a single agent, these clients will turn to that same agent for recommendations in filling the many jobs in the lower echelons. And so the commissions mount.

Packaging also occasionally permits an agent to sell, or rather to unburden himself of one or more items which the studio does not want. Thus the agent can insist on such acquisitions if the studio wants the more desirable parts of the package—the star or the story. Clients are thus benefited, and the studio is saddled with excess baggage which it may or may not use, but which it must pay for nonetheless as part of the package.

The package deal often carries with it a certain amount of internal friction at an agency, particularly in offices that represent not only actors, writers, and directors, but literary materials as well. If a story is decided on as the foundation for a package, embarrassing questions may arise. Which director should be approached, which actor, which writer? Will the choice of one director antagonize another not selected? Will that ill will cause the ignored director to dismiss the agent? These are serious problems of protocol and diplomacy. The same conflict arises when an agent represents more than one producer or executive working at the same studio at the time a story is being submitted to that studio. Which of the clients should be informed, which given the inside track on the project?

Packaging has, justifiably, given rise to a new term, "a creative agent." The agent who adroitly combines a number of profitable elements in a package is, indeed, functioning on an imaginative level. This technique is growing more and more valuable as the dismembered, fragmented, and distraught studios, irresolute and hampered by the inexperience of their new conglomerate proprietors, turn with relief to agents, "creative" or otherwise, to keep their sound stages occupied.

There is an obverse side to packaging, however. Many agents, observing the avidity with which studios are accepting packages, have literally forced themselves upon the studios as producers, resigning from their agency posts to do so. (They have not dared to insist on being directors; that requires genuine talent). Their reasons are arithmetic: ninety percent off the top is better than ten. They are not only selling the package, they are selling themselves. The studio invariably accedes to this *force majeure*, unreasonable though it may be. Hence, there are now dozens—and the tribe is increasing—of totally inexperienced, former agents in charge of productions that cost millions of dollars. Many have never set more than a visitor's foot on a studio stage; their knowledge of picture-making comes from Front Office chatter. Hollywood's low estimate of the importance and value of a producer is in direct proportion to its ready acceptance of this situation. The studio frequently tries to compensate for the agent-producer's lack of ability by supplying him with a "strong" director or a "strong" associate producer or a "strong" cameraman. These are weak buttresses to an indefensible policy. There is no reason why an agent should be a capable producer, or vice versa. Yet the agent-turned-producer can be seen in every studio in Hollywood. The absence of professionalism among many of Hollywood's current producers is notable, and the ready acceptance of agents into the field exacerbates an already worsening situation. A candidate for a producership should be hired on his proven talents, not because he has the control or ownership of a desirable package.

The social status of an agent in Hollywood is clear-cut: he has none. With the notable exception of the corporate heads and vice presidents of some few agencies, Hollywood treats agents as useful, even indispensable, but not as social equals. The number of quips, gags, anecdotes, aspersions, jibes, and denigrations about agents is manifold. No other member of the film industry is so vilified. This invective had its origin in the 1940s when dozens of illiterati invaded Hollywood to enter the lucrative agency field. They were often vulgar, flashy, arrogant, and in some cases dishonest. But though agents still have Rolls-Royces, they are now painted a sombre black. The Hollywood agent who once had his gold-plated telephone rigged so that at the pressure of a desk-button it would slowly and majestically emerge from a concealed recess to within reach of his beringed hand has become a memory. Do not be misled into thinking that the new breed of agents are genteel Phi Beta Kappas (there is *one* in Hollywood), but a number of them now dress soberly, employ the Madison Avenue "soft-sell," and in general comport themselves with decorum. Not all. Hollywood still has the untutored, the unskilled, and the unintelligent among its flesh and story merchants.

Twenty-five years ago agents guilty of chicanery or dishonest representations were "barred from the lot" by major studios for months at a time until the rift was healed. Nowadays a studio that does not "cooperate" with an agent is barred by the agent! No submissions are offered to the offending studio until every potential purchaser in town has first rejected them. And this persists until the disagreement is settled.

It has been said that agents are parasitic in the sense that they derive their strength from the talent and ability of their clients, but the relationship is also symbiotic, for the client depends on the agent. Agents are depersonalized people, for their working and social lives are spent in a continuous endeavor to please everyone. Whatever individuality and identity they may have had before embracing agentry is permanently submerged. They are confidence-men of the highest order, with the producers and executives being the marks. A most successful agent in Hollywood was talking admiringly about his son: "He's a born agent—a real con-man!"

There is a Hollywood phrase, "Blessed are the deal-makers for they shall inherit the industry." This prediction is beginning to take on the semblance if not the reality of truth, and if the industry owners are willing not only to see it happen but to abet it, they will be in a sorry state. Hollywood is in need of showmanship, ingenuity, daring—of genius and dedication. To leave this vital factor in the hands of the agents is improvident, for the majority of them have only one goal in mind and action—to make money for themselves, irrespective of the impact this may have on the industry as a whole.

THE DIRECTOR

*In one way it's very nice . . . but you know we can't go
on forever and not tell our friends and relatives how we
are earning our living.*

D. W. GRIFFITH

Even though directors are being hailed as the saviors of the
film industry (a hope yet to be proven) and there is a growing cult of director worship, the attempt to install the director as the key figure in picture-making and accord him a new
status and dignity is actually a reversion to filmdom's past.
When the motion picture was young, especially during its
silent days, the director was always the most important contributor to a film, but then no one thought of him as having a
personal "signature"; no one used the idolatrous word
"auteur"; nor were such terms as "cinema-stylo," "cinema-
verité," or "neo-realism" applied to his talents; a "director's
touch" went unnoticed. The "retrospectives" which pay
homage to a director's total output and are closely studied to
trace his development as a film artist would have been inconceivable during Hollywood's infancy. Cinematic life was

much simpler and more direct; pictures had to be made and the director was the only one who knew how to make them.

The silent film director operated in many spheres with very little assistance from anyone, nor did he expect or need help. He functioned in every area of film-making: creative, administrative, executive, technical, financial, and even manual. The picture was totally his from concept to conclusion.

When the idea for a film was broached either by him or by someone else, it was just that, an idea, usually a sentence or two embodying a theme or a subject. From that shaky beginning, the director proceeded to concoct the rough outline of the entire film. He rarely committed his unordered action or plot progressions to paper (screenwriters did not come into being until 1908), but rather carried the entire continuity in his head, always subject to instantaneous change in response to the exigencies of the actual shooting. He was also the producer; he cast the picture (occasionally playing a role himself), selected what few crew members there were, budgeted it, designed the simple sets, chose the location, doubled as the cameraman when one was not available, attended to the lighting, supervised the wardrobe, and, of course, was the one and only editor of the rough assembly of film before it was released to the public. In addition, this one-man organization acted as coach and father confessor to everyone on the set. In short, he combined in one person many of the activities of an entire modern studio.

As the need for more films became pressing, company representatives known as supervisors began to appear. Their assignment was to make certain that a specific number of pictures were produced annually to satisfy the demand from the theaters which were springing up throughout the land. This was known as the unit system of production, a method of regulating the flow and quantity of films. These supervisors were the forerunners and prototypes of today's producers. At first they limited their jurisdiction to financial and business affairs, but as they grew in power, they began to inject themselves into the creative aspects of film-making, which had been hitherto left to the director.

It was this intrusion, which shortly became active interference, that prompted the directors to become conscious of their own value and status. Previously they had accepted their multiple responsibilities as a matter of course, but when the supervisors began to treat them as mere mechanics, they resented it. Once the unit system of production became firmly established, the authority and autonomy of the directors began to suffer new encroachments. In essence, they were effectually prevented from exercising the ingenuity and imagination which were their major assets. For example, Thomas Ince, a legendary boss-figure of films in the early 1900s, decided that written photoplays, however skeletal or amorphous, were superior to those fabricated by directors. Thereafter, such photoplays were delivered to the director with the curt instruction stamped on the cover, "Produce this exactly as written." (In those days to produce meant to direct; the words were interchangeable.) Obviously, such a peremptory command robbed the director of any opportunity to effect spontaneous on-the-set inspirations. It was the same Thomas Ince (reported by Lewis Jacobs in his study of motion pictures, *The Rise of the American Film: A Critical History*) who further inflamed the directors with his dictum that "making a photoplay is something like baking a cake . . . you have to have certain ingredients and know how to blend them." A recipe of "certain ingredients" which would be acceptable to both Ince and the director was not easily obtainable.

Another threat to the director's autonomy was the early adoption of the star system by many studios. Stars were what fascinated the public; stars were what the studios were marketing; no one ever attended a movie because of a director.

Studio executives were interested in the director only as the man who took the players through their paces. He was rapidly becoming a technician without recognition or authority, yet subject to censure if the picture should fail.

There were two notable exceptions, D. W. Griffith and Cecil DeMille, but they were geniuses, as much in their profession as in their ability to attract public attention. Both were consummately egocentric; few stars could compete with their deftness in advertising themselves. DeMille, in particular, with his riding breeches, leather puttees, broad-brimmed hat, and swishing riding crop became a towering figure to the public. Apart from these two, however, directors were unknown. They were assigned pictures arbitrarily by their studios, with little regard to their personal interests or desires, and they were very rarely accorded the privilege of editing their own films.

As the industry became more complex, the producer's power waxed as the director's waned. The situation finally became so intolerable to a number of directors that in 1936 forty of them formed a protective union, the Screen Director's Guild, "to check curtailment of the powers of directors . . . on the part of producers." (The organization today numbers 3773—most of them out of jobs!)

It is interesting to recall what their initial demands actually were, since all of them have now been fulfilled:

a) the right to participate in story conferences with the writer and producer.

b) the right to have an active recommendatory role in the selection of the cast.

c) the right to be directly involved in the editing or cutting of the film.

d) the right to participate in final decisions made on the screenplay by the producer.

e) the right not to be assigned a script to direct only one or two days in advance of actual shooting.

These demands seem strangely remote from the present day when the director is fawned upon, charges a king's ransom for his services, and is considered by many studio heads a star in his own right.

The modern director is still the one person (aside from the agent and the financial sponsor) without whom a film could never be made, though he may not be the Jack-of-all-trades his predecessor was. The Hollywood cliché that "movies are a director's medium" is founded on a bedrock of truth. This does not imply that all directors are talented or that all films evolve with distinction or even proficiency because of directors. It means that if any single person is responsible for the making of a motion picture and is accountable for its virtues and defects, it is the director. It is he who coordinates and compresses into a single theatrical unit the capabilities of writers, actors, photographers, musicians, colorists, animators, special-effects experts, costumers, set designers, sound engineers, and so on.

Although written many years ago and patently prejudiced, there is no better description of the value and function of a director who esteems his craft than William DeMille's. In his *Hollywood Saga* he writes:

As a writer I never felt myself so completely identified with the picture as I did when I directed it. I suppose only the director feels the full, one hundred per cent thrill of the movie maker. The picture is his own more than it belongs to any other single person of all the many who must collaborate in its production. He it is who takes all the materials—the story, the sets, the lights, the characters, the actors, the costumes, the make-ups, the properties, and molds them moment by moment into the living thing which is a motion picture. He literally pours himself into the work; not only his art and craft, his knowledge and experience, but also his vitality, his sweat, the hypnotic force by which he welds his actors into that pattern of the whole which is his conception of the picture. He creates the actual thing which the audience sees; no other factor can interpose itself between his work and the public. In some cases editors or supervisors may cut, twist or transpose, but what is left on the screen is still the director's work. That is why the director's sense of creation, even of possession, probably outweighs that of anyone else connected with the picture.

How does the director create this "living thing?" Exactly what does he do? From the crude beginnings of films, it has always been the director's major assignment to suggest movement and development in the images that flash across the screen. It is this illusion of motion, of progression to an awaited resolution, that keeps audiences absorbed, while simultaneously the director endeavors to convey the intellectual (if any), aesthetic (if any), and emotional (if any) ingredients in the story. It is this impression of motion that brings life to the screen narrative; without it, the film loses impact. There are contemporary, experimental films which deliberately defy this premise and depend for their effect on what amounts to a series of still-photos, often purposely repetitive, and these are interesting as exploratory departures from the ordinary, plot-bound Hollywood offering. But such films have little interest for mass audiences and find their adherents chiefly among underground film followers and cinéasts. It is still true that if a film is designed for neighborhood theaters, "it's got to move," as Mack Sennett phrased it.

To sustain this movement without its appearing artificial, to connect individual shots as well as whole scenes, to concentrate upon and underscore the dramatically important at all times, in brief, to hold the film-goer's attention, the director must first have his own conception of the film, a style, a treatment, a point of view toward the project. However, he must also have great flexibility, for he is not alone in creating the film. He must, therefore, also be able to alter and qualify his conception in relationship to the many collaborators he requires.

Unlike the sculptor, the painter, the novelist, the composer, or the playwright, the director has to cope with dozens of disparate elements while still trying to hold to that particular idea he had when the picture was first proposed to him. He must concern himself with the story, the screenplay, the cast, the lighting, the sound, the music, the sets, the costumes, the props—all of which must be given judicious consideration while the film is being made. Nor is his task made lighter by the fact that behind all these components are their human creators, temperamental, egocentric, jealous of their colleagues, protective of their own interests. To achieve balance, to resolve disagreements, to extract the best from each person, is a sizeable problem in human management, demanding extraordinary adaptability and intelligence. A director of merit must therefore be not only a disciplined, knowledgeable, and hard-working professional, he must also be a diplomat. This is especially difficult in Hollywood where respect for sensitive egos, deference to creative integrity, and tolerance of individual psyches are all sacrificed and subordinated to box-office success.

Long before the word "action" signals the beginning of shooting, the director must immerse himself in preparatory work which has little to do with his actual guidance on the set itself. First and foremost is his comprehension of the story. An understanding of story values is a *sine qua non* for a director; he must know whether the story selected is one which can be entertainingly translated onto the screen and can be pleasing (sell enough tickets) to patrons. While it has been said that "anything can make a picture," it does not follow that anyone will want to see the finished product.

Is the story worth doing in the first place? If it is an adaptation, will a screen version improve or impair its fundamental values? Should it be modified or altered for screen purposes, and if so, in what ways? Will such contemplated changes disappoint those who have read it (if it is a book) or seen it (if it is a play)? Are the characters interesting? Will film patrons be concerned with and involved in the sequence of events? Will it attract certain performers? Are the physical problems of set construction or a faraway location too formidable? Is it too costly? All these and many more such questions have supposedly been analyzed and resolved by the producer before the director is invited to participate. But many producers purchase literary material of dubious screen potential, and almost all of them then turn to the director or the writer for solutions. Thus the good director must have a thorough grasp of the intricacies of story construction and its corollary problems before actually directing, and an understanding and appreciation of literature requires a literate and perceptive mind. These qualities are not conspicuous in Hollywood, and most directors are ill equipped to function in the realm of the printed page. They are predominantly visual; they automatically translate ideas and concepts into pictorial images.

Once the basic story has been accepted, the director must participate in the writing of the scenario itself, guiding or misguiding the scenarist in the development of the screenplay. Hence, it is axiomatic that an able director must have some awareness of the problems of the screenwriter. There are a few directors who are capable writers themselves, and they, of course, are of real aid to the screenwriter. But by far the largest number restrict themselves to counselling the screenwriter in broad terms. Their working methods vary: some hover over the writer's shoulder, arguing and advising as each scene is finished; others have lengthy conferences before the actual writing starts and then await delivery of the first-draft, full-length version before suggesting changes. In either case, rapport with the screenwriter and a knowledge, however superficial, of the difficulties inherent in screenwriting are essential. There is and always will be some antagonism between the screenwriter and the director, and the so-called collaboration between the two can hardly be called cordial, a condition which does not make the director's task any easier.

The casting of the picture is another critical step. To cast a picture correctly the director must have reliable information on a number of actors before making final decisions. He must be cognizant not only of their professional abilities but also of their personality quirks. He must know which actors get drunk, which can't memorize lines, which have pronunciation problems, which are late for shooting. Theoretically, the producer shares this burden, but since it is the director who works closely with the actors under daily stress, it is he who must make the ultimate choices—assuming that the Front Office executives will permit him to do so, and that they have not already determined on various players as part of a package.

A director should know a great deal about what the cameraman (or "cinematographer" as the union prefers them to be known) can do. During the shooting and often before each set-up (the placement of the camera and the actors), the astute director confers with the cameraman about the potential value of an entire scene, questioning whether it would be enhanced by being separated into various segments, or whether a long shot, a medium shot, or a series of close-ups would be more desirable. The angle from which a performer is photographed, the use of light and shadow, and numerous other camera deployments can be of significant aid to the director. One who is unaware of the dramatic possibilities in the adroit manipulation of the camera is failing to exploit fully one of the most vital contributions to the finished picture.

A director must be budget conscious at all times. Even though the producer, too, is concerned with this aspect of production, the director has the greater responsibility, since the shooting and staging are under his command and delinquency or delays can cause staggering costs. How many pages can he shoot each day? How expensive will the sets be? How many extras will he require? Can he shoot during bad weather or must he wait for a clear day? Can he transfer an entire scene to a different locale at a saving and still preserve its authenticity and dramatic content?

During the shooting, unexpected crises arise that demand cool judgment, emergencies that could not be foreseen no matter how meticulous the preparatory work has been. For films are made by men, not machines.

Having completed the physical shooting, the director must doff his director's cap and put on the cap of an editor, the more formal name for a film cutter who works together with the director at this point. This is an exacting job; it means long hours in the dark of a cutting room while thousands of feet of exposed film are unreeled and studied to determine where each foot will find its final placement. The importance of editing as a part of the directing process cannot be overstated. "Editing is above all the supreme touch of direction. The two cannot be separated," observes Lee Bobker in *The Elements of Film*. The transposition of scenes, the rearrangement of story continuity, the elimination of tedious passages, the highlighting of others are only a few examples of the wizardry that takes place in the cutting room and often give new and more (sometimes in inadequate hands, less) meaning to scenes.

While shooting, the director tries to control the speed of each sequence, to exact intonations and emphasis in various dialogue sections, to use close-ups or long shots or medium shots for certain effects, to dictate the movements and gestures of the actors, to make sure that the props and sets abet the action and theme without being too prominent. The goal is to preserve the emotional tension, mounting suspense, or comedic interplay of the basic narrative. However, owing to the necessity of shooting out of context and continuity (to save money a director must shoot all those scenes which take place on a particular set one after the other even though they involve episodes taken totally out of sequence), it is frequently impossible for him to achieve emotional and thematic progression from one scene to another, as one can in a play. The fragmentary method of shooting defies consistency; it is only in the cutting room that he can impose coherence. It is only when he starts to piece the film together that he is able to see the picture, disjointed as it is, as a whole. Only then can he try to rectify mistakes in judgment or conceal the disabilities of his performers by shuffling and rearranging the sequences, ruthlessly discarding pointless or repetitive segments, so as not to lose the eye and the ear of the audience.

Most directors are given the privilege of a "first-cut," that is, the right to assemble the film in the fashion they think best. But the director's cut is not final, for it is reviewed by the producer and the corporate employer who can change the director's arrangement—and they generally do. There have been occasions when a director has asked that his directorial credit be removed from the picture, feeling that the version being shown does not fairly represent his conception of the film. This highhanded usurpation of authority is another illustration of the corporation's disregard for its employees as craftsmen in their own right. For no matter how desirable the director seemed before being hired, once he has finished his first-cut he is dismissed from the picture, and many a director's interpretation of his film has died in the cutting room. In too many cases the director's first-cut is little more than a minor courtesy.

The most immediate and most significant part of a director's work lies in his relationship with actors. Oddly enough, the average director regards actors at best with tolerance and at worst with active aversion. Many a director has expressed envy of the Disney studio where animators and cartoonists make films without actors. There is a privately held belief among directors that most actors are mindless puppets, which view, since a good proportion of directors were once actors themselves, carries a certain authority.

However, there are valid and less querulous reasons for the director's negative attitude toward actors. For example, an actor has a difficult time developing either an emotional or an intellectual comprehension of his part because the scenes are so disconnected as he performs them before the camera. This is not his fault, but it makes it hard for him to achieve fluidity and ease in his performance. Nor is he always able easily to understand his role in relationship to that of the other actors. It is only the director who can envision all the roles and their values in the script as a whole. Moreover, there is no audience as in the legitimate theater to provide reactions to the actor, to serve as a gauge for his interpretation. At least the director is there in lieu of an audience. But perhaps the most substantial reason for the director's disparagement of actors is that the majority of Hollywood actors are "personalities," not disciplined performers. The cult of the personality will be discussed later, but it is mentioned here because it heavily influences the director's opinion of his cast.

Antonioni, a great director who has worked with actors from various countries, is quoted in Lee R. Bobker's *The Elements of Film* as saying:

> *It is not possible to have true collaboration between actor and director. They work on two quite different levels. The director owes the actor no explanation except general ones about the character and the film. It is dangerous to go into details. Sometimes the actor and the director necessarily must become enemies. The director must not compromise himself by revealing his intentions. The actor is a kind of Trojan horse within the director's citadel. I wonder whether there exists a really great film actor; what a great film actor would be like. The actor who thinks too much is troubled by one ambition: to be great. This is a terrible obstacle, and it carries with it the risk that his playing may be deprived of much of its truthfulness. . . . Sometimes an actor is intelligent enough to overcome his limitations and discover for himself the proper path to follow—that is, he uses his own intelligence. . . . When this happens, he has the qualities of a director.*

Hollywood actors are indeed often petulant, unreasonable, and vainglorious, which is perhaps why Peter Brooke, a distinguished English director who has worked on both sides of the Atlantic, once told a London *Times* interviewer that, "One should never praise a good actor; but always blame a bad one."

On occasion actors themselves admit that the director controls their fate. John Wayne, who has kept the lucrative loyalty of his public for more than a quarter of a century, has said that as far as he's concerned, "there's always been one boss on a picture, the director. I haven't always agreed with him, but I've paid attention." There is good reason for

Wayne's healthy respect: on occasion he has played the role of director himself, always with sorry results. In several of his attempts, an experienced director was hastily summoned to salvage what he could.

In general, directors avoid saying anything in public about actors for obvious reasons. Despite the talk of the New Hollywood's no longer needing name actors, the actor of prominence remains in a commanding position. Directors may have attained importance in recent years, but there are —and always will be—actors who have the contractual right to choose their own directors. Hence, the reticence of most directors to express any derogatory opinions which might be repeated.

There are a few directors who have cheerfully and successfully selected, trained, and used the services of people with no theatrical experience of any kind. While this is done most frequently by European directors of the neo-realism school, there are a small number of directors in Hollywood who have also taken "unknowns" and put them in leading roles. Whether they choose to do this because of their distrust of the professional film actor, as characterized by Antonioni, or because they desire to play Pygmalion is an unanswerable question; the fact remains that untrained people have occasionally achieved transitory fame under the guidance of capable directors.

There is no doubt that, as producer-executive Milton Sperling has said, "The director has become a key ingredient in insuring the studio of its investment." This is confirmed by Richard Zanuck: "The director is really the maker of the picture." "In our marketing of American pictures the director's name has been so established in the minds of the public that he has become a major box-office asset for any picture he directs," wrote George Sidney, for many years President of the Screen Director's Guild, in the *Motion Picture Herald* as far back as 1962.

Such recognition may have given directors delusions of grandeur, but it has also prompted them seriously to reassess their position in the industry, to question the hitherto accepted "indispensability" of their traditional collaborators, the writer and the producer. If the director is "really the maker of the picture," and if his employers attest to it by high salaries and flattery, it is small wonder the director asks why he should share the glory and the dollars with men he considers creatively inferior. If directors are recognized by the industry as being completely responsible for the film, why shouldn't they have complete control?

Foreign directors of repute and achievement have long felt they should. "Creation must be total for the director from beginning to end. I'm convinced that the present failure of Hollywood is because of this. To divide, in art, is not to conquer"—this from director Jean Renoir (quoted in Ezra Goodman's *The Fifty Year Decline and Fall of Hollywood*). Many of the more rebellious and experimental younger American directors, joined by a number of veterans, have decided to take on the duties of the producer or the writer along with their own. In some cases they have undertaken the triple vocations of director, writer, and producer. Their first attempt has been to eliminate the producer and give the director the encompassing title of director-producer. Certainly the director who clings to the hope, however forlorn, of introducing some element of artistry into his film considers the producer to be his enemy. For in the current repressive climate of the conglomerate hegemony, it is usually the producer who is most obedient to corporate mandates.

The absenteeism of producers has also helped to widen the rift between directors and producers. With the current decline of the Hollywood studio as a base for production, it is far from unusual for the producer to sit cozily in Hollywood or London or Paris while the director is off on a rugged location, coping with the many problems of actual film-making. This is an irritant and an affront to the director, for the producer's absence does not prevent him from bombarding the director with cables or phone calls when he does not like the "dailies" (the total footage shot in one day) which are shipped to him by air express. Not only has the director shouldered a sizeable proportion of the pre-production tasks, but now he has the producer looking over his shoulder long-distance. And the producer's name will appear prominently on the screen as the creator of the finished film. Stung by vanity as much as by its inappropriateness, the director has always taken strong exception to the producer usurping credit for what the director has largely accomplished on his own. "I made *Wuthering Heights*," Samuel Goldwyn is credited with saying, "(William) Wyler only directed it."

To directors like John Sturges, the producer is more an encumbrance than an aid. In an interview appearing in Paul Mayersburg's *Hollywood: The Haunted House*, Sturges said:

> *I think the pictures that have been made by directors who have become producer-directors are better on an average than they were when they worked solely as directors. I know it's a more satisfactory way of working. I like to consider myself a picture-maker more than a man who directs in the strict sense of the word. . . . I like doing it by myself. If I'm wrong then I'd like to be totally responsible for being wrong.*

Stanley Kramer is quoted by Mayersburg as endorsing this viewpoint: "it helps a director . . . if he can become his own producer because it cuts down front-office interference, not entirely but somewhat." Kramer goes on to discuss the so-called creative producers, but even here he doubts whether assistance from such a source is of value: "Since the director is the hub of the picture, there will always be difficulty if you have a creative producer unless there is tremendous team-work and rapport. So by and large my feeling is that the emergence of the producer-director for top creative people has been a very wise thing." Whether it's a "very wise thing" or not, it has become accepted in the New Hollywood. Among the hundred and fifty or more such producer-directors in Hollywood are William Wyler, Alfred Hitchcock, and Otto Preminger, and the number is rapidly increasing.

There are other directors, equally disenchanted with the traditional roles, who have elected to merge their directorial activities with those of the writer, but who leave the administrative supervision in the hands of a producer. The designation of writer-director is new, but it has long been thought that a director might also be capable of writing for films.

Before the writer and director merged, it was customary for directors to compose supplementary material that was not in the basic screenplay, or to alter it by deletion or modification. This "writing," however, usually took place only during shooting and did not necessarily include putting the changed words down on paper. It is also obvious that a director's choice between a cut or a close-up may markedly affect a story point, giving it a different impact or impression than that intended by the writer, a form of directorial "rewriting" that annoys screenwriters. But then any literary contribution from the director, either by scene alteration or actual writing, has been resented by writers. Their spokesman is Garson Kanin (in Leo Rosten's *Hollywood: The Movie Colony—The Movie-Makers*): "Anybody can direct a good picture if he's got a good script."

The writer has always lamented that his screenplay can be changed, even mutilated beyond recognition, once it is entrusted to the director. The admiring critical words "that's the director's touch" are deeply resented by writers who say that the "director's touch" was nothing but a carefully written screen-direction in the screenplay. Writers have consistently claimed that the only way to protect a screenplay is to direct it oneself. Thus, from the writer's point of view, too, the advent of the writer-director is looked upon with considerable favor.

In further defense of the director's decision to become a writer as well, it is a fact that the writer often presents scenes the director considers unshootable, or writes directions into the script that jeopardize the fluidity of movement the director is seeking. William DeMille makes this point in *Hollywood Saga:*

> *If the writer is too exact in defining every move of the camera, every cut and every angle, he robs the director of freedom in his own proper field; he ties the director's hands to the point of cramping his cinematic style and preventing his use of the camera as an instrument for emphasizing dramatic values instead of merely recording action.*

It is natural, therefore, that the director, feeling constrained by the screenplay, and the writer, despairing at the license taken with his manuscript, should prefer the two functions fused into a single creative process. As of 1971 there were 166 writer-directors, whereas some five or six years earlier there was not one tenth of that number. Among them should be mentioned George Seaton, Haskell Wexler, Ralph Nelson, and Melville Shavelson.

What with some directors having become director-producers and others writer-directors, the next combination was the triple-threat man, the writer-producer-director, what Martin Ragaway in his "Hollywood Dictionary" defines as "a man who has only himself to blame." This fusion of talents is nothing new in Europe where the man who undertakes it is labeled "auteur." The "auteur" is really a modified version of the old-time silent-film director. The European "auteur" selects the story, writes it himself or in collaboration with a screenwriter, directs the film, and in many instances supervises every mechanical detail including optical effects, laboratory work, and the final release prints. The American writer-producer-director is also involved in all these processes to a greater or lesser degree and includes such men as Billy Wilder, Daniel Arnold and John Cassavetes. A less clumsy appellation than writer-producer-director is "film-maker," a term which has become popular in the New Hollywood.

Motivating the film-maker is his desire for a personal signature. The director knows that film production demands many hands and brains (the hearty Hollywood term is teamwork!). Nevertheless, he believes that by removing some of his collaborators, such as the writer and producer, he can come closer to realizing his own ideas in a film. "Think how very few American films, even among the good ones, have a signature," John Houseman wrote in the magazine *Film Quarterly*. "There is a very strong resistance to individual statements in American pictures, while among the worst European film-makers there is nearly always some kind of personal statement."

This ambition to preserve the integrity of a single creative imagination is admirable. However, can the film-maker as an autonomous artist succeed in Hollywood? Is he really autonomous because he is the writer, producer, and director? Can he make a personal statement in his film? Or does the "very strong resistance to individual statements in American pictures" still persist in the New Hollywood? Will a corporation really entrust any one man with absolute creative power —which ultimately means financial power—on a project costing millions of dollars, even if it grants him the title of writer-producer-director? Can this happen under our current system of production and distribution? The answer is no! The triple-threat man is valiant but doomed. His authority is an illusion. If all he is seeking is the gratification of personal vanity by an impressive title, he may be satisfied. If, however, he is seriously interested in making pictures that reflect and embody his personal convictions, he had better make certain in advance that his convictions are acceptable at the box-office—and there is no way of doing that.

Samuel Fuller, who has pondered the roles of writer, director, and producer over a long career and who has tried to give his films a "personal signature," comments that, "95 per cent of films are born of frustration, of self-despair, of poverty, of ambition, for survival, for money, for fattening bank accounts; that's what's behind 95 per cent of films. I think that five per cent, maybe less, are made because a man has an idea, an idea which he must express."

It is impossible to imagine the giant industrial conglomerates that now own Hollywood ever entrusting their financial fate to any group of writer-producer-directors, no matter how brilliant or dedicated such film-makers might be. Though a modest number of them have broken through commercial barriers and won a devoted cult audience, their influence on the industry as a whole is negligible. The commercial film, the film that draws large audiences and consequently large profits, the bread-and-butter film, is the lifeblood of Hollywood and any departures from it will remain deviations from the norm. For every distinctive and individualistic picture the triple-threat men make, there are hundreds of others which will follow tested audience formulas and which film-makers must also direct if they wish to survive.

In the *Los Angeles Times* of November 5, 1970, Noel Black (one of the new film-makers) remarked: "We're a lot closer to the Hollywood of 1935 than we are to the Utopian film world that everyone has been saying is right around the corner. . . . I don't think things will be turned over to the creative people all that easily." Dennis Hopper, of *Easy Rider* fame, quoted in the same issue, added:

> *There's still a lot of the same old kind of thinking around. . . . The only thing the studios have to offer a young film maker these days is their distribution machinery. . . . I suppose the reason the studios got so powerful is that lots of directors think they don't know anything about business. I'm not sure if I know anything about business or not, but I do believe that they don't know anything about art. And if they're in business and don't know anything about art, they're not going to let art take their money.*

Another young film-maker, Robert Downey, said, "I think the one thing guys like myself have to watch out is not to become as corrupt and safe as the people we've fought against." And Jim McBride said: "Whether the Hollywood system, the capitalist system is good or bad, whether it lets young film-makers do what they want or not, is not the point; it seems to me a terribly outmoded system based entirely on greed, encouraging the most evil kinds of motives while discouraging the most lofty ones."

Pictures cost money; they're manufactured to make money; personal statements have no place in Hollywood unless they make money, and the few exceptions prove the rule.

The writer-producer-director will survive, perhaps even multiply (from the corporate viewpoint, the remuneration is considerably less than the total fees that would have to be paid to three separate individuals), but he will not be encouraged to make quality films any more than when he was merely a director. Not unless the whole pattern of Hollywood financing is changed. Writer-producer-directors who assume that by absorbing all three operations they can circumvent the mediocrity enjoined by their employers are foolish. If the signature on their films is personal, you may be sure that it has been endorsed by the corporation.

Parenthetically, not all personal signature films, even those made outside the United States, are worthy. The assumption by one-man film-makers that complete control assures a cinematic masterpiece is nonsense. Whereas films made under a single aegis have the advantage of a single driving force behind them, the quality and competence of that force are variables. Moreover, even one-man film-makers cannot function in isolation; they, too, require the cooperation of other people. A film will always suffer from or profit by those supplemental contributions.

Until mass audience taste improves, it is the average, the banal, the familiar, the "safe" film which will be made. Risk pictures or prestige pictures (sometimes known as flops *d'estime*) are pictures made because some impassioned film-maker has persuaded a nodding studio head of their possible box-office (not artistic) value, but these will always be exceptions. Occasionally a prestige picture will be sponsored by an otherwise commercially oriented studio head in order to mollify a particular director at a particular time. Usually, however, it is only because the director simultaneously agrees to direct one or more films of the "safe" variety. The bow to quality is more than compensated for when the same director signs a contract agreeing to oversee other films which the corporation favors.

Whatever the frustrations and affronts to artistic authority, there are always many people ambitious to become Hollywood directors. How does one become a director? The film industry, stupidly, has never made any effort to educate its craftsmen, directors included. Hollywood lives in the present. Thousands of university students now major in the cinema arts and are interested in directing, but they will find little encouragement when they present their credentials at the Hollywood studios. Sporadic attempts have been made to initiate apprenticeship programs, such as are commonplace in almost every other large industry in the United States. But again and again, either through apathy on the part of the host-studios or because of active hostility from the self-protective unions and guilds, these programs have died. Now and again an individual producer or a studio will grant a six-month scholarship to a student, but this is far too infrequent to be of much value; and once such a student has concluded his brief tutelage (which consists largely of being a spectator-attendant during various phases of the development of a film), he is on his own. No job is offered; no future is promised.

The lack of an organized program to train prospective applicants for industry posts is patently detrimental to aspiring directors. Consequently most Hollywood directors come from other sectors of the entertainment field. Many trace their professional beginnings to the legitimate stage, where they were actors. In the early, union-free days an actor could easily cross over into directing. The New York theater still provides Hollywood with film directors, but nowadays they come largely from its stage directors. The major problem in transplanting these stage-trained directors is their ignorance of the camera, but this obstacle is not insurmountable.

In Old Hollywood, many directors were ex-cameramen who were often given the opportunity to direct secondary scenes. Others spent hours in the editing or cutting rooms, rearranging film to help directors get the effects they wanted. This directing-with-a-scissors involved close collaboration, allowing the editor to expand his knowledge to a point where film editing became an avenue to directing. In those days there was another way to learn the director's trade. Every studio produced a number of short subjects, "fillers" played in conjunction with the feature pictures, which enabled some currently notable directors to master their craft and get sufficient experience to embark on full-length films. Short subjects are still made in Europe and still provide a superb educational and practical background for many fledgling directors; they no longer exist in Hollywood.

Another former source of directors, now vanished, was the dialogue director—invariably men from the theater world who were in large demand following the introduction of sound. They were imported from Broadway and elsewhere to teach silent-film actors how to talk. They advised on regional pronunciations and speech eccentricities, tried to obliterate speech defects, worked on the purification of idiom, tested for sound volume, directed rehearsals in the absence of the director, and in general, acted as the director's alter ego. Dialogue directors are rarely found nowadays; most film directors will not tolerate their presence, considering them a nuisance on the set.

Assistant directors are seldom given the opportunity of becoming directors. This failure to advance their own craftsmen is strange, but Hollywood has always been notorious for seeking talent outside its own backyard. In addition, there is a maxim which says that good directors are good because their assistants are better, which may explain why directors do not promote the ambitions of their assistants.

The most productive source of directors today is television. Qualitatively they leave much to be desired, but that does not bother Hollywood; it likes their shooting methods, which involve the filming of all scenes very rapidly and economically, thus saving time and money. Another reason why television is a fertile ground for contemporary film directors is its accessibility to Hollywood executives. It is far simpler for them to turn on their television sets and watch a director's technique than to leave their offices or houses for the theater.

Other directors come from the ranks of the screenwriters. Any writer of proven ability, meaning a long record of produced screenplays, can use *force majeure* to compel a studio to let him direct his own screenplay. He does this by being the owner of a book or play or screenplay which a studio covets; his asking price includes the right to direct it. Studios rarely succumb to this pressure willingly; they do so only if the executives cannot get the story on any other terms. In Paul Mayersburg's *The Haunted House* he quotes the successful director David Swift, who, when asked for advice on how to become a director, replied: "I broke in because I was a writer and controlled the property . . . and the only way anyone could get it or do it was to take me along as a director. So if any young would-be directors ask that question about how to break in, the answer is invest your money in properties." "Invest your money in properties" is good, salutary counsel, but usually impossible to follow. Most writers are not that rich.

An overly casual answer to the question of how to become a director is provided by Richard Rush, himself a former writer and now a director of some fame. In the April 1970 issue of *Action*, Mr. Rush says, "If you want to be a director, direct . . . the things that cost the most in a studio— actors, sets, scripts, etc.,—are free to amateur film makers. They can get their friends to perform as actors and crewmen and use real locations for nothing. The only cost is cameras and film." Apart from the fact that Mr. Rush rather cavalierly dismisses the price of cameras and film, his recommendation is hardly contributory to getting a job in Hollywood. This same Mr. Rush, interviewed three months later in the *Los Angeles Times* (June 14, 1970), was a bit less idealistic when he remarked: "Despite the enormous changes in the industry there's no avenue really open to make it as a director. Somebody's still got to put a million and a half in somebody's hand. Somebody's got to risk an enormous amount of money."

With hundreds of directors collecting unemployment checks from the state of California, the prospects for newcomers are dim. Barring nepotism, always a key to Hollywood's door, there is no easy entry into the world of directing. No textbook can be written on "How To Become A Film Director."

Even those New Hollywood directors who have reached the pinnacle of their profession take orders from the Front Office, or from so-called independent producers who obey the instructions issued by the heads of the owning corporations. There is little difference between venal Old Hollywood and venal New Hollywood. If a director does not believe that his major value to the studio is commercial, his naivete is beyond credibility. In assessing directors, Joseph Levine, the President of Embassy Pictures (a conglomerate subordinate), epitomized the Hollywood viewpoint in an interview reported in *Variety* of August 19, 1970. Discussing directors who might deserve to be called great, Levine concluded with feeling and conviction: "Mike Nichols is the greatest director ever in films. Why? Because he never had a failure!" Levine was speaking for the industry.

Now, a mild word for the "bosses." The prevalence of *kitsch* and the absence of taste that characterize many Hollywood films are not uniquely the fault of the bosses, though much of it is. Many directors look upon their profession as a strictly commercial, highly paid trade; to them "art" is as much a mystery as it is to their employers. An enormous proportion of the 3773 directors on the roster of the Screen Director's Guild do not pretend to be artists; in fact, they are astonished by the sudden respect for what they always considered a pleasingly gainful occupation, but nothing more. In *The New American Cinema*, edited by Gregory Battcock, there is an article by Charles Boultenhouse, "The Camera As A God," which puts this quite honestly:

> *The Hollywood director is usually surprised to discover that his "art" has been taken seriously; this is because he has never been serious about "art" as such. His first concern has been to make his film as exciting as possible in order to keep the customers coming to see it, so that the investment would be protected—yield a profit. A Hollywood director, plainly speaking, is a craftsman using all his skills to protect an investment by making as much profit as possible. If his skills and devices are repeated and developed to the point where they can be identified, this does not make him into an artist. . . . When it comes to the total work of these efficient imaginative craftsmen, one must simply face the facts. Their films cannot be studied as a developing revelation of artistic intention, not because their skills did not develop, but because they never had a single artistic intention, and it is pointless to pretend that they did. The truth is that the commercial director should have the proper and honest reward of being credited with a job well done rather than wear the dubious appellation of "artist."*

The successful poet, novelist, sculptor, or painter in modern times usually has a hard time getting to the top; nor is he paid much along the way. The director, even the one who is most voluble about creating a masterpiece untarnished by commercialism, ordinarily travels in style. Few directors even begin thinking about a proposed film project until they have a signed contract with adequate remuneration. The number of directors who invest in their own films is few. The Screen Director's Guild is a union, not an eleemosynary institution.

Let the director call himself what he will: writer-director, producer-director, writer-producer-director, auteur, filmmaker; if he wants to work in Hollywood, he will manufacture films that can make the greatest profit with the smallest expenditure of money. Whether he does it willingly or reluctantly is not the issue. All directors, young and old, idealistic or opportunistic, will by and large make films that cater to audience tastes, and neither art content nor personal statements tend to loom large at the box office.

A few words for those cinema lovers who believe that the contemporary crop of directors, unhampered by censorship and striving for "personal signatures," will defy the commonplaces and emancipate the industry. They are particularly impressed with the New Hollywood's courtship of young directors as opposed to veterans. Even though these young directors represent but a minor fraction of the hundreds of aspiring directors, they are sufficiently vocal and have become sufficiently publicized in the New Hollywood to warrant more than passing attention. In the first place, where did they come from? How were they able to penetrate impregnable Hollywood? There are many answers, but they can all be subsumed under the frantic desire of the new owners of Hollywood to cultivate youth audiences, and their further belief—or better, blind faith—that young directors, mainly because they are young, are aware of what young film patrons want. They further assume that a disregard of previous filming methods, a wholesale repudiation of past techniques, is an additional way to attract the youth audience. And so the conglomerate owners are seeking directors who are young. They come from Madison Avenue commercials, television, from the making of stag pictures, underground films and amateur films.

Several admonitions are in order. The first is that a youth audience is not only mercurial; it grows up and its tastes change. The second is that in trying to lure youthful patrons, the film industry has divorced itself almost completely from its middle-aged constituents. The third point is that untried directors who jettison previously successful subjects and time-tested filming methods do not automatically create interesting films. The novel is no guarantee of excellence.

No more need be said of the youthful directors unless it be the statement of Martin Rackin, a confessedly middle-aged producer and former studio head. Asked about the advantages of hiring young directors, Rackin commented in *Variety* (July 1, 1970): "How would one feel on a plane if he heard the announcement, 'Good afternoon, this is your pilot. I'm Irving Schultz, 17.' Or imagine being operated on by a 19-year old surgeon."

In summary, neither Hollywood executives nor most of its directors have any concern with film as an art form, unless it leads to a profit. Should American audiences change and flock to those few theaters presenting films with superior artistic and ideological values, Hollywood will promptly change as well. Hollywood is not against art on principle; it is only against art if there is too small a market for it. If such a market becomes bigger, Hollywood directors will be the first—urged, commanded, by their employers—to move into these new avenues, or rather, new revenues.

Hollywood has always been dominated by fear of commercial defeat. That fear is even more prevalent in the New Hollywood, led as it is by industrialists who are neither showmen nor creators. It is this fear that overcomes all filmmakers, and it is one to which directors, who are principally responsible for the finished films, are more subject than anyone else in the industry.

THE STAR

*I got all the schooling any actress needs. That is, I learned
to write enough to sign contracts.*

HERMIONE GINGOLD

Are there any real actors in Hollywood, or are they merely
marionettes made to move by directors? Is there any important difference between the Hollywood actor and the stage
actor? How important are glamour and sex appeal? Is intelligence a requisite for good acting? What is the effect of public worship on a Hollywood actor? What are the factors that
elevate an actor to stardom? What *is* a star? Are stars made
or born? Does the star system exist in the New Hollywood?

It must be said immediately that the majority of successful Hollywood film actors are not serious actors, they are
"personalities." A "personality" is a player who has attained
marketable fame quite apart from any artistic ability he may
have. If such an actor has talent as well, the asset is welcome
but unnecessary. Personality actors are not born; they are
manipulated into stardom. This manipulation is accomplished, first, by technical virtuosos whose legerdemain is
applied to the face, figure, hair, voice, walk, stance, and ges-

tures of the actor; and second, by gigantic publicity organizations which grind out endless copy, see that the actor gets exposure through film magazines, television, and radio, arrange ballyhooed personal appearance tours, and encourage the establishment of world-wide fan clubs.

There is probably no other profession in which the cult of personality is so dominant and yet so patently artificial in its origin. America has other heroes, mainly in sports, and recently it has discovered its astronauts, but they are unimpeachable, proven performers. Their accomplishments are not the result of calculated artifice. The athlete and the astronaut who become objects of public adoration are truly experts, leaders, front-runners in their own fields of endeavor. Similar fanfare, propaganda, and press-agentry are used to enhance the exploits of these folk heroes, but such campaigns are always *post facto*. The athlete or astronaut has already demonstrated his ability before the publicity mills begin to grind. He does not need to be invented; he exists. This is not true of a Hollywood "personality."

In addition to the publicity that helps create and sustain the Hollywood personality actor, there are a number of outside forces which establish and support him: the director, the cameraman, the make-up man, the sound engineer, the cutter, the lighting technician, all of whose skills and technical equipment account for a disproportionate amount of the so-called performance that appears on film. The Hollywood "personality" is a fabrication, part talent (sometimes), but principally the result of the artful employment of other professionals.

Ivor Montagu in *Film World* makes this distinction between a personality actor and a real actor.

In the late twenties a distinguished Japanese actor visited London. The members of the Film Society had just admired an exquisite Japanese film—the first to be seen in

Europe—a highly stylized classical legend. It was natural, therefore, to ask the visitor, thru an interpreter, if he ever appeared in films. The answer was a grunted monosyllable. The interpreter translated: "Mr. X says,—in Japan only those actors appear in films who cannot sing, dance or act."

This does not mean that Hollywood personality actors "cannot sing, dance or act"; indeed, a number of them can do all three. It means that hundreds of Hollywood actors succeed with only minimal ability as actors or entertainers. Many an actor has been genuinely surprised, when, as part of an audience, he sees his finished picture for the first time. Of course the audience believes what it sees and assumes that the actor intended it that way. It is the rare actor whose personal interpretation of a role is so commanding and authoritative that he transcends all external supports, giving us something rooted in his own perception and sensitivity.

As has been stated earlier, it is the director who must fully comprehend the various roles in a film, and who advises the actor on how to speak his lines, what gestures to employ, how to stand, walk, run, sit, and lie down, how to respond with a shrug or a frown or a smile, when to move and when to be still. The actor may and occasionally does have ideas of his own, but the personality actor is usually delighted to subordinate to the director any conception of the role he himself may have. By so doing, the actor avoids friction and protects himself from criticism of his work by making the director responsible for it. Most actors don't like directors but are only too happy to obey them. An intransigent actor may fret, but in the end he will do as he is told, for the director represents the corporation eager to make a successful (box-office) film, and the personality actor is conditioned to follow any path leading to that happy ending which will augment his reputation and his salary.

The actor is guided by other professionals as well, all of them of prime importance in forging his final performance. The most valuable of these is the cameraman. His discretionary use of various angles, positions, and deployments of the camera are extremely important. His decisions on the length of exposure time may make startling changes in the scene. The long shot, the medium shot, the zoom, the iris—all produce different impressions on an audience, heightening or reducing interest, concentrating attention when desired and diverting attention where it could be superfluous or harmful. The close-up, in particular, if adroit, can be of tremendous moment, especially when the actor cannot deliver his speeches with sufficient emphasis. For actors who are lip-lazy, the close-up can be a boon of another kind, encouraging or supporting his professional slovenliness. In her *A B C Book*, Marlene Dietrich notes that, "The film actor has an easier time if he chooses not to articulate; the audience's ability to lip-read during close-ups helps the ear."

The manner in which an actor is lit, how lighting is used to project shadows or brightness, not only conditions what the viewer sees but affects the style and method of the performance as we see it on the screen. The sound engineer, who can mute or modify or amplify certain words and speeches, occupies an important command post. Many an actor has found his own voice eliminated from the finished film and the more pleasing or more appropriate voice of another actor substituted on the sound track. And this is done so dexterously that the public is never aware of it. The make-up man is another technician at the service of the actor. He conceals wrinkles, covers facial defects and skin discolorations, hides puffy eyes, and provides hairpieces to disguise baldness. It was Marlene Dietrich who also remarked, "The relationship between the make-up man and the film actor is that of accomplices in crime."

After the filming is completed and long after the actor

has finished his engagement and departed, the shoring up continues. At this point the cutter takes over with his editorial shears. A skillful cutter is the *deus ex machina* of films. Lengthening or shortening scenes, removing or substituting speeches or parts of speeches, and rearranging the sequence of action can all significantly alter the actor's interpretation.

All these men and machines function without any but the most superficial cooperation from the actor. Listen to a sound engineer discuss an actor's voice, or to a make-up expert analyze an overly prominent nose, or to a cutter scrutinize a particular gesture—one might easily think that the actor was made of plastic. They almost never mention his talent. Their activity is centered on his voice, face, eyes, movements, not on the man himself. They might prefer an actor who has some professional skill, so that their tasks would be less arduous; but whether such skill exists or not, they conduct their operations with only perfunctory reference to dramatic ability.

Whether a Hollywood actor needs to understand the script, the parts of all his co-actors, or the subtleties of his own role, are questions often debated. Are actors just "tall children," as the Hollywood joke has it, who are more comfortable if they are manipulated by the director, the public relations experts, and the technicians? Many actors find such questions irrelevant. What concerns them is whether the audience likes them, which, in turn, means their bosses will. If the public and the producers are satisfied, the actors are satisfied. Once a "personality" has the public's stamp of approval, the studio is more than reluctant to let the actor tamper with his audience image by changing his style. The successful "personality" is an asset; why risk it? Producers are fully aware that acting talent is not essential for a "personality." Beth Day, in *This Was Hollywood*, notes that

Howard Hughes responded to a query about the dramatic ability of his star Jane Russell (she of the magnificent mammaries) by observing: "There are two good reasons why men go to see her. Those are enough." Though George Bernard Shaw was talking of the stage, his remark about actors is applicable to the screen: "I do not want actors and actresses to understand my plays. That is not necessary. If they will only pronounce the correct sounds I can guarantee the results."

There is one real danger in all of this. Even actors with taste and ability may be lulled (or gulled) into accepting themselves as "personalities" rather than actors. It is a hard thing to lose the public's affection and loyalty once you have had it.

It has been said that most Hollywood personality actors are really re-actors; that is, they re-act and respond without providing any initiative of their own. (Even those actors who are artists tend to relax their professional standards in Hollywood.) Being re-actors instead of actors makes the work day less onerous. Such an attitude of almost total dependence on external, artificial assistance is a denial of the actor's identity as an artist, but this does not disturb him, though "artist" is sprinkled throughout his contracts.

John Wayne is a staunch defender of both the anti-artist concept and the actor as a re-actor. In Charles Hamblett's *The Hollywood Cage*, Mr. Wayne says:

> *There's too much pretentious nonsense talked about the artistic problems of making pictures. I've never had a goddam artistic problem in my life, never, and I've worked with the best of them. . . . I read what's in the script and then I go out there and deliver my lines. The director knows what he wants from me, and he gets it. I don't have to have nine or ten takes before they get*

something they can print. . . . I don't go around shooting off my mouth about the problems of acting. In fact, I don't even call myself an actor. I'm a re-actor.

Teachers of acting know how hard it is to make Hollywood performers take the profession seriously. Stella Adler, a disciple-teacher of the Stanislavsky Method, has said that the actor can never really master his craft as long as he is in Hollywood films. As quoted in the *Los Angeles Times* of June 21, 1970, she told her class to "Forget about this rotten moving picture quality you develop in this rotten town. Forget it! Who cares if your eyebrows are on straight? . . . Acting is doing. You're paralyzed until you understand this."

Even if the would-be actor in Hollywood wants to solve some of the "goddam artistic problems" John Wayne belittles, he is hard put to find anyone in Hollywood to guide him. Except for a few fly-by-night institutions which cheat him, there are no schools of merit. Organizations like Stella Adler's are rare, and the goal there is the stage rather than the screen.

At one time all the studios maintained competent teaching staffs for new players, but these drama schools have long since been shut down and their coaches discharged. Another fine training ground was lost when short subjects disappeared, those one-to-four-reel films formerly manufactured in great quantity. In addition, every studio at one period produced a number of what were called "B" films (made on very modest budgets) which also offered experience to untutored talent. These too are now part of Hollywood history.

The abolition of traveling stock-companies which once roamed the land on one-night stands, the disappearance of vaudeville, and the virtual elimination of legitimate theaters in many cities have drastically reduced the number of places where actors can learn their craft. There is little left of the stage except Broadway (inhospitable and inadequate as that is), off-Broadway, and the regional theaters, and the latter are facing the crushing pressure of steadily diminishing funds so that their survival is in doubt.

Television is the main source of supply of new film actors, as of directors. It may be said to have replaced "B" pictures and short subjects as a school for actors. But since television actors get even less training than do feature film players, and since the production time-pressure of television is acute, slipshod work is commonplace—"After all, what's the difference, it's only for TV!" George Cukor commented on television as a training ground for actors in the *Daily Variety* Anniversary Issue of 1970: "They are lucky if they don't stay in it long and if they don't learn."

University acting schools, well-intentioned though they are, are usually so remote geographically or psychologically from the commercial world of Hollywood that they are of almost no value in recruiting screen actors. Few colleges have made any effort to bridge the gap between their amateur courses and professional requirements.

Here again, the Old Hollywood had something that has been lost. When it was dominated by Louis B. Mayer of Metro Goldwyn Mayer and others of his kind, it spent large sums to groom its recruits. The actors of that period may not have been superior to today's, but there was at least some organized effort made then to educate actors before they faced a camera. It was George Cukor again who said:

Sometimes you see people and you say "that person might really be something" and you wonder where in hell they will learn. . . . I think, "if Mayer were around, that person would be a big star, maybe the first rate or the second rate." He would develop them. They [studio heads of the Golden Period] *cared, and they were or-*

ganized, and they knew how to do it. To-day, you see, they haven't got the faith in their own destiny, the people who are running the studios.

Working against the likelihood of Hollywood actors taking their profession seriously is, of course, the inflated self-esteem that comes from living in a world of fantasy, surrounded by sychophants and parasitic flunkies. It was the actor Robert Morley who said, "Actors live in a cocoon of praise. They never meet the people who don't like them." Even uncomplimentary notices are somehow twisted into near-adulatory comments. "As long as you spell my name right, I don't care what you say about me."

This "cocoon" existence is protected by the immense sums paid actors or "re-actors" or "personalities." "Let's face it," said James Garner, "actors are paid more than they're worth. Producers are idiots for paying what we ask." Shirley MacLaine, quoted in *Films and Filming*, was equally vehement: "When I see the amount of money flung into that cauldron called Hollywood, I feel not one ounce of guilt about what I get. Producers have always grumbled about the money they pay us, but they keep coming back."

Underlying the actors' demands for high salaries is the gnawing fear that one day the golden flood will cease. In Hollywood fear is omnipresent, and being "available" (jobless) is the greatest fear of all. Even a stupid actor knows that his reign may be short-lived, that his public is fickle, that the studio will repudiate him the moment his popularity dims, that competitors are waiting for him to fail, that a young star grows old, that the cornucopia of Hollywood is not bottomless.

Taxes are unwelcome to most of us; to the Hollywood actor they are a personal affront. One method used to minimize taxes is for the actor to incorporate himself, taking advantage of the corporation tax which is lower than that levied against an individual income. Another method is to "spread" a salary over a long period of time, thus permitting the actor to enjoy a form of self-purchased annuity or pension. A third method is to become a "bona fide resident of a foreign country . . . for an entire tax year," a Treasury Department ruling (originally instituted to protect Americans working in remote areas under hazardous and difficult conditions), exempting a percentage of the actor's income from all taxation. A number of very highly paid actors have established residence in Switzerland or Spain and use pressure tactics to have any film in which they appear shot where they reside. Another way of sheltering money from the tax collector is to acquire a part ownership in a film through a participating interest in the profits. The actor who tries this takes care to protect himself against a non-profit picture by receiving in advance a sizeable portion of this potential profit in lieu of salary. The more ingenious changed even this formula as soon as they discovered to their discomfiture that some of their pictures never made a profit. They now exact a share of the gross receipts, irrespective of the film's success or failure. Other compensations which are becoming less prevalent as the Internal Revenue Service becomes more attentive are "gifts" from studio executives of automobiles, boats, and houses.

The salary of a successful actor is by far the largest item in a film budget and frequently means the difference between profit and loss to the producer. But such matters are of no concern to many actors, who are not interested in the picture (other than whether it enables them to demand larger fees for the next one), or in the financial health of the film industry. Their interest is utterly self-protective and if "idiot" producers continue to agree to pay fantastic prices, actors will demand them. And since a celebrated actor is a form of insurance for the studio, every effort is made to please him. A successful actor is still king of the Hollywood jungle.

One status dividend an actor often requests is the right to name his director and frequently his producer too. An important actor can also demand changes in the screenplay: dialogue revisions, elimination of certain characters, additions to the actor's own part, reduction in the size of other actors' parts, supplemental scenes, and so forth. Rarely does an actor ask for a script change which would benefit the screenplay as a whole, without reference to his part. Again and again, an actor will accept a role after having read the screenplay and then make unexpected demands for drastic revisions. These requests for revision often come only after the actor has signed his contract and the studio has made its salary commitment to him. An actor may use his power to select cast members whom he favors or he may insist on a favorite cameraman, who may be more expensive and less competent than the one designated by the studio.

Actors who are subject to tantrums, superstitions, and neuroses of all kinds, real or imaginary, find Hollywood an ideal place. The studio will do everything in its power to humor the "tall child" to avoid jeopardizing its investment. Actors ask for and get masseurs (to tranquilize their jangled nerves), chauffeured cars to drive them to and from the studio, special hairdressers or makeup men, portable dressing-rooms on the set to prevent fatigue, stand-ins who are personal friends, provisions against cutting or restyling their hair, private secretaries, and more. There are some actors who require that tea be served on the set at 4 P.M. every day, or that the temperature on the stage be maintained at a certain degree. Some have a 5 P.M. quitting time in their contracts which they honor whether or not the director has completed the takes for that day. Starting dates of films have been postponed—a most expensive procedure—because a

star's horoscope deemed the chosen date inauspicious. Inno-
cent studio employees have been known to lose their jobs
because a star was annoyed; in one actual case, a script girl
who wore a purple dress was removed from the picture because the actor told the director he was allergic to purple.

Billing on the screen, in newspaper advertising, and on
billboards is another point of friction. From a reading of the
standard actor's agreement it would seem that no such controversy could ever arise. This clause reads:

> *Provided the Artist appears recognizably in the Artist's
> role on the film on the Photoplay as generally released,
> Producer agrees to announce the full name of the Artist
> as the first star on the film of the Photoplay and in all
> paid advertising issued by or under the control of Pro-
> ducer to advertise the Photoplay. In according such
> credit the full name of the Artist shall be announced in
> first (1st) position among the entire cast of players above
> the first mention of the title of the Photoplay and size
> (both heighth and width) of type at least as large and
> prominent as that used to announce the title of the Photo-
> play. The name of no other person whose services are
> utilized in and in connection with the Photoplay shall be
> announced in type larger or more prominent than the
> type used to announce the name of the Artist.*

But suppose the producer later contracts for another star
whose billing demands equal or even surpass those of the
original star. Disagreements arise as to the precise size of the
type in which an actor's name will be printed. What, for
example, is the exact meaning of "prominent"? Are free
handbills announcing the film "advertisements"? In the event
that the title of the picture is printed in small type, will the
actor be satisfied with type "at least as large and prominent,"
or will he complain to his agent that he is being demeaned?

Where there are a number of actors in a picture, all of them important, the billing imbroglio can become agonizing. Once in a while a harried producer is permitted to bill all actors alphabetically, but this is rarely approved by actors. The billing battle will continue as long as producers are subservient to their actors, and they will be as long as the actors are the money magnets of the box-office.

The temperamental, self-indulgent actor is not a Hollywood fiction; he is a reality. And if a celebrated actor is denied his demands, he may give a slovenly, dispirited performance (known as "walking through a part"), which can destroy the picture's chances of being a success.

Although we have been concentrating on the actor in Hollywood, it seems advisable to devote some space to the differences between the film actor and the stage actor. Most Hollywood actors eschew the stage even though they may owe their initial reputations and present status to its influence and training. Those who return now and then "to do" a play on Broadway are usually of two kinds: the few who respect their craft and wish continually to perfect it; and those who are failing in Hollywood and desperately hope to be "rediscovered" in a New York play.

Most film actors are simply afraid of the stage, afraid of being exposed without the protection of friendly cameramen, sympathetic sound-mixers, flattering lighting experts, understanding make-up men, and indulgent cutters. They are reluctant to depend on talent alone to sustain them in front of an audience. Hollywood offers much more money for a few months work than they could earn in a year's run of a play on Broadway. In films the actor's salary is guaranteed whatever the box-office fate of the film; on Broadway a play may open and close in twenty-four hours, leaving the actor out of a job. If a film actor "blows" (forgets or distorts) his lines, the scene is shot again and again and again until an improved reading has been obtained. Such indulgence cannot exist on the stage, where mistakes sound the death knell of the play as well as of the offending actor.

The screen presents no opening-night tensions; a film premiere is a gala social occasion for publicity, and critics have long before judged the film in the comfort of studio projection rooms. Nor does the fate of a picture hinge on the criticism of a handful of drama reviewers, as does a Broadway play. Although there are thousands of film reviews distributed by print or electronic media, only the New York critics can affect a film's and an actor's future. Yet in terms of box office, the New York critic's influence is limited to Manhattan; adverse reports on films emanating from New York have very little effect on the rest of the country.

Hollywood caters to an actor's indolence; the daily shooting permits him to relax between takes or even to be absent while sequences in which he does not appear are being shot. The theater actor—with rare exceptions—must be in attendance either on or off stage during all performances. Quite simply, he works harder, and under less pleasant conditions. Compare the sunlit, swimming-pool ease of the West Coast and a New York hotel in sweltering summer or rigorous winter.

Fundamentally, all the reasons that deter a Hollywood actor from braving Broadway are founded on fear—fear of smaller remuneration, fear of inability to function without props, fear of critics, fear of climate, fear of environment, fear of hard work, fear of audiences, fear of his own inadequacy.

The small number of actors who occasionally do a New York play actually find the experience stimulating and rewarding. They find satisfaction in an audience's responses, for there is never any contact between the film actor and his public beyond personal appearance junkets and autograph seekers. However, even those Hollywood actors who essay the stage out of respect for the theater are careful to sign self-protective contracts limiting their stay in New York to a specific period of weeks, regardless of the success or failure of the play. Allegedly to guard against going stale in the part, the real reason for these short-term contracts is to keep the actor available for Hollywood roles, and Hollywood salaries. The number of actors who undertake the three thousand mile journey to work in the New York theater remains unimpressive. It is much easier to be a "personality" (and a well-paid one) in Hollywood.

Any examination of actors in Hollywood leads ineluctably to the stars, or the "tallest children" of all. It is ironic in this era when hard-pressed Hollywood is seeking ways to counter their power, that the Hollywood of some sixty years ago likewise made every effort to prevent the star system from infiltrating the industry. Until 1910 or thereabouts, the leading players in films were presented to the public without their real names. This anonymity was deliberate. Some famous players were known only by the corporate name of the studio for which they worked: The Biograph Girl, The Vitagraph Girl, The Imp Girl. Others had their identities concealed behind the parts they usually played; for example, G. M. Anderson, the first cowboy star, was known to his fans as Bronco Billy; Gladys Smith (Mary Pickford) was called Little Mary. As the popularity of these actors and actresses increased, curious admirers began writing letters asking for their real names.

For a time the producers resisted; once the public learned the names of the performers, the popular players would be in a strong position to demand more money. But the letters asking for the players' identities continued; and Carl Laemmle, the head of IMP, a flourishing company of the period, decided to break the deadlock. He acted not out of interest for the public or benevolent concern for the particular actress involved, but as a way of assuring her exclusive services. Laemmle persuaded Florence Lawrence, then at the peak of her success as The Biograph Girl, to leave that studio and affiliate with him. He not only promised to pay her more money, but more important and precedent-breaking, to emblazon her real name on all her films and in all the studio publicity. Rival organizations quickly copied Laemmle's daring maneuver. The star system was born.

Player anonymity vanished in a series of talent raids throughout the entire industry. Laemmle capped his conquest of Florence Lawrence by luring Mary Pickford and her actor husband Owen Moore to his organization. Vitagraph, a competitive company, did the same with Florence Turner; and by 1911 there was even a dog star named Jean, heretofore known only as The Vitagraph Dog.

Almost simultaneously the salaries paid to players, now stars, skyrocketed. By 1916 Charles Chaplin was receiving $10,000 a week from the Mutual Company, and the remuneration of other stars likewise escalated to dizzying heights. Three years later the star system received a further boost when three stars and a director formed their own company. These four were Mary Pickford, Douglas Fairbanks, Charles Chaplin, and D. W. Griffith. To the producers of that era their defiance was the ultimate in ingratitude. "The lunatics have taken charge of the asylum," was the comment of Richard Rowland, then head of the Metro Company. Today we again have corporations owned and controlled by individual stars.

Once the public was able to identify the objects of their worship, Hollywood used every device to increase this devotion. The first "movie palace" was erected on Hollywood Boulevard, renamed The Avenue of the Stars. Sid Grauman's Egyptian Theatre was built in what his detractors called "early Frankenstein" style. Criticism did not trouble Grauman or his patrons, who flocked to see films in the new imposing Temple of Art, as Mr. Grauman called it. Some five years later he built The Chinese Theatre on the same street, the stone flooring of which still bears the footprints of past and present stars as well as the nose of Jimmy Durante, the profile of John Barrymore, and the hooves of the horse that belonged to Gene Autry.

The Hollywood star is a phenomenon of the twentieth century. Millions of people avidly follow the public and private lives of the stars, imitate the gait, the manners, the gestures, the clothes, the speech, the hair style, the eccentricities of the favorites. They will hearken to pronouncements from the stars, and even elect them to high political office. No one knows precisely what makes a star. Charisma, sex appeal, glamour, vitality, youth, and beauty all seem important, but there are stars who are not young, not beautiful, not glamorous, and devoid of sex appeal. Only one thing is certain; talent is not an essential ingredient. Said Samuel Goldwyn, whose films were invariably star-studded, "God makes stars. It's up to the producers to find them." Said Marilyn Monroe, "Only the public can make a star . . . it's the studios who try to make a system of it."

Whatever the derivation of a star may be, Hollywood has learned that the star is the core of the film. The film is structured around him in every possible way. This does not mean that the other actors do not contribute to its audience impact, or that the other components of the film are unimportant. But the star is the intermediary, the conduit through which the audience receives its primary impression of the picture. As Nicholas Schenck said when he was President of Metro Goldwyn Mayer, "There's nothing wrong with this business that a star worth $10,000 a week can't cure." "Put the light where the money is" was and still is the studio's instruction to the cameraman and the director, and that means directly on the star.

In 1962 Richard Schickel wrote in *The Stars,* "The star stands at the very center of movie economics, and it is to his public image that all movies, no matter how high their artistic aim, are tailored." Ten years have passed, but that statement is still valid.

Making a star is an intricate, demanding process, one which the Old Hollywood had organized to an extraordinary degree. When Metro Goldwyn Mayer had sixty players under exclusive contract and boasted that it had "More Stars Than There Are In Heaven," the finding and grooming of stars were vital. Fan mail was carefully analyzed; popularity polls were taken, letters from theater managers were given scrupulous attention. Hollywood was alert to any sign of public interest in a player. Once it was ascertained that the public's affection was more than a passing fancy, it was cultivated by press-agentry into a full-blown love affair. Although Hollywood has always prefered to invent and perfect its own stars, it functioned just as ably when audiences made their own choices. The "discovery" of a potential star by audiences was, however, often a craftily planned maneuver by a particular studio. The number of stars found accidentally among drive-in car-hops or soda fountain waitresses was, and still is, minimal.

During the Golden Period every studio had complicated techniques for developing a star's charisma. This process invaded every corner of the player's daily life. No player was permitted to be interviewed by any publication without an alert publicity agent in attendance, whose assignment was to deflect embarrassing questions and prevent the player from making awkward statements that might impair his image. Wherever possible the player's social activities were tailored to fit the image of stardom. Romances, marriages, parties, friends, restaurants, clothes—all were dictated whenever possible. Nor did the stars object, for they knew the cash value of the image. Stars were not people, they were properties. Louis B. Mayer often described the financial stability of his studio by saying: "We are the only company whose assets all walk out the gates at night!" In 1945 Twentieth Century Fox interviewed some 90,000 aspirants throughout the United States, and hundreds were given screen tests. Paramount spent nearly $2,000,000 a year seeking and training potential stars, or "starlets," as they were then called. Studios were equipped with physical therapists, dentists, medical doctors, orthopedists, cosmeticians, diction coaches, dramatic teachers, talent scouts, dancing and singing instructors, and even high school and elementary teachers for children who were star timber. The discipline was rigorous; indolence or delinquency were not condoned. Becoming a star was a joyless process. Disobedience resulted in contract cancellations. Player and studio alike took the task seriously.

Publicity staffs were organized with specialized departments to service the daily papers, magazines, radio, national columnists, local columnists, and gossip purveyors. Publicity "stunts" were the order of the day.

But today, in a cost-conscious era, star-making as an elaborate, encompassing, institutionalized operation has been virtually abandoned. As players are no longer under exclusive long-term contract to major studios, the initiative has diminished for the studios to spend time, money, and effort on creating public images for them. Independent producers do not have the means to indulge in extravagant publicity campaigns or to surround their players with the complicated training paraphernalia that major studios once employed. And yet the power of a star is more significant in the New Hollywood, and more critical to these independent producers than ever before. Without a star they often cannot get a release or distribution for their films. So essential is a star in today's market that a new term has entered the Hollywood vocabulary, a "bankable" star.

One knows a star is "bankable" only after meticulous study and analysis of the national gross receipts of the various pictures in which that star has appeared, a close examination of audience popularity polls, of the reactions to the star by exhibitors and theater owners, of the revenues from foreign engagements, of the volume of the fan mail. When these figures are correlated, the star is deemed "bankable" or not. If the tally is affirmative, any number of banks which service film companies will loan large sums on the strength of the star's name. They will not lend money on the basis of a screenplay, director, or producer, except in the most unusual conditions. The "bankable" star is the best collateral.

Fortunately for producers in the New Hollywood, stardom can be created much more rapidly nowadays owing to the multiplicity of publicity media and the swift diffusion of all information. Previously, potential stars were led through a "leap-frog" system: an obscure player was groomed for stardom by being paired with an already famous star in a series of pictures. The new player would thus be seen by the large audiences loyal to the established star, and would simultaneously, it was hoped, attract a following of his own. At the same time the publicity machines would disgorge propaganda about the newcomer. This no longer happens, but the exposure offered by television is infinitely more effective in providing a weekly audience of millions. What once took months and sometimes years can now be accomplished in six months or less.

It is true that television's prodigious output of film may result in a number of its "personalities" being *over*exposed to such an extent as to invite audience boredom. This danger is real, but it is more than compensated for by the audience's ability to achieve an intimacy with TV stars as a result of this very frequency of contact. A considerable number of "personalities" have made the leap from TV to Hollywood, and the quantity is increasing; television has proven again that the public craves stars. The producer-writer Andrew J. Fenady, addressing a film class at UCLA, said ". . . if by some stretch of the imagination the industry would eliminate a star system by regulation, the public would create a new one immediately. I keep hearing that the day of the big star is gone and will never come back. That's hogwash!" In other words, the first question asked about a picture is still "who's in it?" And for those few starless films which have attracted large audiences, the most repeated query heard among the exiting patrons is "who was so-and-so?"

One of the evidences of the New Hollywood's bondage to the star system, despite any protestations to the contrary, is the deliberate use of the word itself in a variety of combinations wherever legal restrictions do not interfere. Thus we not only have films with stars; but we also have "co-starring," "also starring," "guest stars," "special guest stars," "cameo stars," and "introducing new stars."

The major objection to stars on the part of the film industry today is not that they are difficult to find, difficult to train, or difficult to cope with, but that their salaries are ruinous. The profit participation formula mentioned earlier in which the star receives a percentage of the profits offers only a temporary advantage to the conglomerate—that of not disbursing a large amount at the initial stage of the venture. Hollywood's new executives tried to eliminate the star system *in toto*, perhaps heartened by the success of a few pictures without famous players. But any monetary advantage gained from these few starless films is cancelled by succeeding pictures with the same leading players, for the vaulting salary demands of previously unknown players who were "discovered" and acclaimed are already approaching the figures paid former Establishment stars. And these demands are reluctantly but consistently being met by the same inexperienced moguls who clamor for low-budget, starless films. The current popularity of certain films without celebrity names is a phase, not a trend, and these are usually foreign or avant-garde films rather than those shown in the neighborhood theaters. Films destined for mass audiences still work best if there is a star.

Since actors are the heart of films, since their audiences and their employers have substantiated this in every possible manner, since the professional and public behavior of actors can be of incalculable influence, it might be assumed that the stars would use their authority to challenge some of the inequities and vices of the medium which pays them so well. The number of actors who refuse roles on ethical, moral, social, religious, or political grounds are not many. A few have exploited their celebrity status to espouse national or local causes, and they are to be admired. But within Hollywood itself their only manifestation of concern has been to improve their own economic status, exempting only generous donations of time and money to the Motion Picture Relief Fund, of which they, too, are beneficiaries.

Star-power tends to corrupt. To be a star is to live in a world insulated and apart from life itself. Dustin Hoffman, a star of this New Hollywood, said it in an interview in the *London Sunday Express*:

> One of the main things about being successful is that I stopped being afraid of dying. I was always obsessed with death, obsessed with things ending, my career being finished. Now I'm not so much. I couldn't understand why that was for a long time, and finally I realized it's because when you're a movie star you're already dead, you're embalmed.

THE WRITER

Each book purchased for motion pictures has some in-dividual quality, good or bad, that has made it remarkable. It is the work of a great array of highly paid and incom-patible writers to distinguish this quality, separate it, and obliterate it.

EVELYN WAUGH

Hollywood writers have been praised and pilloried, re-spected and reviled, but no one has disputed the uniqueness of their position in the writing world. Hollywood itself seems to regard them as considerably better than common clay, for in common with the other "artists," writers are referred to in studio contracts as having a "special, unique, unusual, ex-traordinary, and intellectual character involving skill of the highest order." Actually, however, the screenwriter is looked upon by studio management as a necessary irritant, an adjunct to film-making, to be tolerated and discarded as soon as possible. The screenwriters, in turn, consider the adminis-trators to be tyrannical ignoramuses whose major purpose in life is to smother the creative ability of writers. "Give a producer a pencil and he'll cut your throat with it" best describes the writer's attitude.

The writer who leaves New York publishing for Hollywood finds himself subject to conflicts, pressures, edicts, and restrictions which he never knew existed before. He experiences affronts to his integrity, his working methods, his creative idiosyncrasies, and his autonomy. Perhaps for the first time in his career he ceases to be master of what he writes. Unwanted collaboration is forced upon him. He must cope with a number of often illiterate bosses instead of a single literate editor. He cannot prevent the words he writes from being changed by directors, actors, producers, executives, and—worst of all—by other writers. He has no control over the film which is the finished product; he is often anonymous to the audience; he does not "write" a script, he "knocks it out"; and he learns that screenplays are not written but rewritten. The talents that prompted Hollywood to hire him may be called upon to subvert another man's work. He may just have written a novel or play of striking originality, a work which brought him to Hollywood's attention; he may have arrived in Hollywood still glowing from the praise of reviewers, audiences, or readers; but he soon discovers that his proven ability is of little interest to his employers.

He is not asked to write an original story for the screen. On the contrary, he is discouraged from doing so. For the screenwriter is engaged primarily to alter the work of others. He is employed as an adaptor. His job is to translate a novel or a play or a work of non-fiction into the medium of the screen via a screenplay. Or he may be ordered to supply new dialogue for a screenplay already written, and instructed not to change the "structure"; in brief, he is not to be creative. In either case, he finds himself compelled to use the ideas, plot, characters, and imagination of some other writer.

And in this humble role he has absolutely no power. He

is told what to do, and in many instances, how to do it. His advice will be sought, his objections discussed, but in the end he must compromise with the expediencies of the film medium and his employers. He swiftly becomes aware that he is a hireling whose value lies in his ability to subordinate his own talent to another. In short, he is no longer a writer; he is a screenwriter.

The screenwriter is also confronted with another imposition peculiar to Hollywood. Hollywood is myopic; it can only see his latest accomplishment. As a result, the assignments he gets are in the category of that latest accomplishment. If a man has written a successful mystery, he will be expected to rewrite mysteries; if a comedy, comedies. He is automatically and arbitrarily typecast, as much as any actor. Nor does his classification change except under unusual circumstances. It is rarely suggested that he might like to venture into other kinds of writing. He is labeled an expert in one style and form.

The story department in every studio has a cross-filed card index on writers that would make Linnaeus's *systema naturae* seem the jottings of an amateur. Writers are divided into categories: action, animal, biographical, documentary, comedy (sophisticated or knockabout), costume drama, emotional drama, melodrama, horror, light romance (presumably as opposed to heavy romance!), murder, mystery, musical, religious, science fiction and fantasy, sport, spectacle, suspense and intrigue, war and service, Western, and a wide array of others. Once a writer has made his mark in one of these fields, he is captive. That becomes his exclusive domain, in spite of any protests he may make.

The only way for a screenwriter to indulge his own creative fancies is to initiate a story for the screen which is completely his own, what is known in Hollywood as an "original." But he rarely does this. It is the jobless writer who writes an "original" in the hope of marketing it to a producer.

The employed screenwriter would never attempt it, for everything he writes while on salary belongs to the studio that employs him. No Hollywood writer owns the material he writes; he writes to order or he does not write at all.

The film industry does everything in its power to discourage "originals." This discouragement begins with the stories purchased for the screen. The industry concentrates on story material which has already attained recognition through prior publication or, in the case of a play, prior production. This practice, of course, eliminates any serious consideration of "originals," for they have had no such public exposure or testing. Hollywood is afraid—and this is only one of its many fears—afraid to trust its own judgment or even its own experience. By accepting the choice of a book or magazine publisher or a play or television producer, the studio heads feel that they have substantially reduced their risks. The fact that someone else has taken the initial financial gamble gives Hollywood a sense of security, mistaken though it may be. Well over 85 percent of the stories that reach the screen are developed by, and come from, communication media outside the film industry.

This reliance on opinions from outside the industry determines what producers choose for the screen. Producers have only one overriding criterion in story choice, as in every other aspect of film making—will it make money?—and since over the years the acceptance of other people's convictions has provided them with the most satisfying answers, they see no reason to change. Nor are they troubled by the fact that this fidelity has made the Hollywood film notable for mediocrity. Dwight MacDonald once observed: "It is very different to *satisfy* popular tastes, as Robert Burns' poetry did, and to *exploit* them, as Hollywood does." The demands of commercialism determine, in large part, the quality of stories chosen for the screen, and the screenwriter has no choice but to accept this reality.

In filmdom's infancy, there were no writers as such. Screen stories were either concocted by an imaginative director or founded on "story suggestions" or "picture ideas" which were bought for nominal sums. A typical price for such a suggestion or idea in the early days was $5 to $15 (the price paid for *My Fair Lady* was $5,500,000). These "picture ideas" were often repetitive, with the same plot or "gimmick" (central idea or notion) offered again and again to an unsophisticated public. So prevalent was this practice that at one time the Warner Brothers' story department, typical of those at all studios, was known as "the echo chamber." The word "screenwriter" was unknown; the few men who put words to paper were called "constructionists," because their job was to design a skeletal structure upon which the director (who might himself be the "constructionist" of his film) could elaborate.

Being indolent, lacking creativity, or both, the constructionists soon realized that there was an abundance of picture ideas to be found in the world of print. Since this was a period when protective copyright laws were laxly enforced, these "writers" pirated and sold (for very small sums) numerous stories from the literature of the past, and the film company heads were delighted. This profitable business came to a halt, however, when the flourishing Kalem Company illegally appropriated Lew Wallace's *Ben Hur* for films. A successful suit was jointly instituted by General Wallace's estate and the publishers of the book, and Kalem was forced to pay $25,000. Writers as well as producers began to realize that they could no longer help themselves to anything in print. A new era came into being and with it a new use for what came to be known as the "screenwriter." Now that story material had become a calculable item in the budget of a picture, the commercial values inherent in the purchased story had to be maintained in the screen version.

The question of the applicability of stories to the screen

has always been a formidable problem for the film writer. When he is hired to write a screenplay version of a novel or play, he is confronted with a *fait accompli*; he does not participate in the choice of the story. His opinion is not solicited. If he finds the material unmalleable, his only recourse is to reject the project—which means not getting the job. Such rejections have occurred in the past, when jobs were plentiful, but they are almost nonexistent today. It is only the writer of exceptional integrity or equally exceptional solvency who declines an assignment nowadays, even though he thinks the story offered him is beneath contempt and beyond repair.

Writers have always criticized the producer's reasons for buying a "property." They are convinced that such decisions result from an unreasoned worship of "best sellers" or "smash hits" rather than from a careful analysis of the film possibilities the property offers. Writers know that this often inflicts adaptation problems on them which are as intolerable as they are insoluble. They understand, even if their employers do not, that just because a story is in print and well liked by the public does not guarantee that it can be "licked" or shaped into a successful screenplay.

The competitive method of offering properties for sale bears out the writers' complaints. As has been noted, the submission of literary material to would-be buyers in films permits a simultaneous presentation to all studios and to all producers. There is a terrifying pressure, therefore, to read a manuscript and decide on its merits as quickly as possible, so that a rival cannot acquire it. This frenzy has led to the institution of the "story analysts." These are highly trained, literate, skilled readers whose job it is to reduce the mass of literary material submitted by agents, publishers, producers, authors, relatives, and friends to synopses of from three to twenty-five pages or more. Because of the need for a swift decision, it is not unusual for a story to be purchased solely on the strength and validity of the short précis that some story analyst has extracted from a five hundred page novel. The producer-purchaser frequently does not read or analyze the novel to ascertain its screen potentialities until *after* the purchase has been made.

In Hollywood's Golden Period, this synopsis-system flourished at all studios, but Metro Goldwyn Mayer added its own peculiar refinement. It had a storyteller on its payroll whose duty it was to narrate orally to the eleven executives who made the ultimate decisions the story under consideration. These men did not even read the synopsis, let alone the book or play. They based their final judgment on a "telling" of the story, and one of them achieved fame among writers by evaluating many stories with the remark, "Take out the essentials and what have you got?" This Scheherazade method is no longer used, but the synopsis method still prevails.

Few producers in the New Hollywood, and fewer of their conglomerate leaders, seem to regard story selection as of vital significance. If mistakes of judgment are made, it is the writer's job to correct them. That's what writers are for. Few cinema rajahs would agree with Samuel Goldwyn, quoted in Paul Mayersburg's book, *Hollywood: The Haunted House*:

> *I was once asked, "What do you think is the indispensable requirement for a good picture—the star, the producer, the director or what?" I answered, "the author." A great picture has to start with a great story. Just as water can't rise higher than its source, so a picture can't rise higher than its story. The bigger the stars, the director and producer, the harder they fall on a bad story. It is the ubiquity of the "bad story" that encumbers and impedes the screenwriter whose task is to make it into a*

"good story," meaning one that will attain profitable acceptance on the screen.

Although the screenwriter is now an accepted and integral part of the industry, the battle for recognition and identity was long fought. It was not until 1933 that the Screen Writer's Guild came into being with an initial roster of 150 members. It was officially recognized by the National Labor Relations Board in August of 1938, and in 1954 it affiliated with the Television Writers of America and the Radio Writers of America to emerge under its new, all-inclusive name of Writer's Guild of America, West. As of 1972, it had some 2900 members.

Of these nearly 3000 writers, very few began their careers in motion pictures. Of the entire membership, it is safe to say that not more than 3 or 4 percent learned their trade in films or did their first professional work for the screen. As has been said before, Hollywood has little or no belief in its own judgment in the selection of story material, nor has it in the choice of its writers. It prefers to draw its literary talent from among those who have achieved fame in other entertainment and communication areas, largely from the theater or from publishing. An Open Sesame to a writing job in Hollywood is a successful play or a popular novel.

Years ago, there were sporadic attempts by individual studios to train new writers from among university and college students who showed talent, but the experiments were short lived; Hollywood rapidly returned to the standard practice of hiring writers from other fields of literary endeavor. Those colleges that maintain screenplay writing courses today do so with the full knowledge that their students may well find no jobs in Hollywood.

Yet the lure of films continues, and the desire to cross the Great Divide between New York and Hollywood persists even though the migrating novelist or playwright soon discovers how difficult it is to accept the loss of his independence. He finds it hard to comprehend the indifference shown by his employers to his personal tastes and abilities. He finds himself nostalgically envious of the liberty and latitude he enjoyed as a freelance writer. For the novelist or playwright or poet has the privilege of being completely responsible for his work. It is all his; he stands or falls by what he has written. At no time is he subject to any pressure on what to write, though he may get advice from his editor or agent or play producer. This is not true of the screenwriter: he is subject to strictures from employers whose taste and judgment he may deplore; he has no voice in selecting the story he is to rewrite; and in addition he is exposed to pressures of other kinds. The dialogue which he carefully tailored to the ability of one star may require drastic revision to suit another who was not even considered when the project began. Budgetary requirements enjoin severe limitations on the script writer. Flaubert spent six weeks writing twenty-five pages of *Madame Bovary*; Hollywood writers have deadlines to meet, production dates to consider, and they labor under a moral and sometimes contractual obligation to deliver from ten to twenty-five pages weekly. In addition, they must be familiar with international, national, state, and local censorship codes, even in our permissive era. If the film is destined to have its greatest appeal abroad, the amount of dialogue must be limited and the story line or action used to convey the meaning. Actors with speech idiosyncrasies or short memories must be catered to, the star and the director placated. The writer must always bear in mind that his words are meant to be spoken, not read. As a diverting sidelight, some of the most literate prose in a screenplay is often found in the stage directions, for here the writer is subject to no supervision; here he writes eloquently—for six people to read.

If by some chance, some or all of the executives in charge of a film are changed during the preparation of a script, the writer too must change his style and sometimes the content of the script. In brief, the screenwriter is engaged in a cooperative enterprise; he is not writing to please himself.

The more consequential and meaningful the original book or play is, the more difficult it is for a screenwriter of taste and conscience to alter it for the screen. His employers expect him to retain the "story values" (revealed to them by the synopsis), simplifying the ideas to accommodate the mass audience. In the case of a first-rate novel the screenwriter is tortured by his appreciation of the literary values embodied in the work. He faces a secondary dilemma too, for in trying to preserve the quality of a distinguished book he contributes little or nothing of his own artistry. On the other hand, if the work is literary trash he can try—if his employer permits him—to inject something fresh or original into it. But here again he is likely to encounter an obstacle, for the second-rate book was probably bought for those very qualities the writer finds most meretricious.

The screenwriter's problems are not confined to the original work to which he is assigned. Since the screenplay is the blueprint for the entire picture, everyone connected with the production is involved in its transformation into film, and the screenwriter is at the mercy of any of a number of technicians. Even the most superior screenplay can emerge as a travesty of the writer's original intent because everyone engaged with the making of the film uses it for his own purposes. Too often, instead of working together and fusing into a single unit, the individuals making the film clash, and inevitably it is the writer's contribution that is the most seriously affected.

In a profound sense, this raises the question of whether

or not a Hollywood screenwriter, hampered and frustrated as he is, can claim to be considered an artist, a designation that he covets and that a good novelist or playwright has the right to enjoy. It has been said by many critics that the moment a screenwriter undertakes the remolding and restyling of another man's work he becomes nothing but a carpenter in words, a journalistic repair man, and hardly merits being called an artist at all.

Frank Pierson, a director-producer, has expressed this point of view in *Films and Filming*:

> *I think that writers in cinema have been suffering too long under the delusion that a screenplay is a work of art. The work of art isn't the screenplay; the work of art is the finished film, and the screenplay is only one element in it. Fundamentally, the screenplay could be considered as nothing more than a list of props for the prop man to assemble; a list of sets for the art department to build; a list of lines for the actors to memorize; and a set of instructions to the director about who, where, what, how and why. But when you go beyond that, the screenplay is really nothing. It bears as much resemblance as a blueprint to a finished building.*

In contradiction to Mr. Pierson, it can and must be mentioned that a number of screenplays and the films made from them are clearly superior to the third-rate novels or plays that inspired their adaptations. All in all, it seems inadvisable to make comparisons between adaptations and their original source material since each is a separate composition; each has its own format, approach, technique, and purpose; each is addressed to a different audience; each has its own consciousness and its own viewpoint; each has different restrictions and demands. To condemn a screen transcription of a novel on the grounds that it is impossible to capture on film the essence of a book may be as unjust as to assert that the adaptation creates a new work which should be evaluated on its own as an individual, expressive form.

The screenwriter should be evaluated by a more precise yardstick than whether he adapted someone else's work or supplied the original concepts himself. Many screenwriters have demonstrated that their craft can be a challenging one, requiring great skill. To translate or transform from one medium into another, from verbal images to visual images, is no mean task and should not be deprecated. The word "adaptor" is by no means a pejorative term. Of course, one of the major difficulties in judging the merits of the screenwriter's contribution is that he is not responsible for the finished product, the film itself. The screenplay is merely a means to an end. Film patrons will approve or disapprove of the final film and give little or no attention to the screenplay which initiated it. In that sense Margaret Kennedy, as quoted by Hortense Powdermaker in *Hollywood: The Dream Factory*, is correct: ". . . there is really no such thing as screen *writing*. A script is not meant to be read, as novels, poems and plays are read. It is no more a work of literature than is the recipe for a pudding. So long as the meaning is grasped, and the recipe followed, it would serve its purpose if it were written in pidgin English."

Screenwriters may object to Miss Kennedy's describing their efforts as "the recipe for a pudding" and her reference to "pidgin English," but they cannot challenge her statement that "a script is not meant to be read," and therefore cannot be evaluated on its own. For unfortunately, it has no life of its own. Only those people—and they are few indeed—who are familiar with the basic literary material *and have read the writer's screenplay* in addition to viewing the picture are entitled to judge the screenwriter's contribution.

Unhappily for the screenwriter, even the most brilliant screenplay filled with dazzling word-play or profound ideas takes second place on the screen to what is absorbed visually. An extremely experienced screenwriter can of course suggest various images via the directions in his screenplay, but in ninety percent of the cases it is the director's intelligence and dramatic sense that ultimately create the visual environment. And it is this total environment that forms one's judgment of the film. Thus, although the screenplay is the bedrock of a Hollywood film, its position continues to be anomalous, as does the screenwriter's. "This is a fine script," one director said enthusiastically, "a marvelous script. I *know* I can fix it!"

So clear-cut is the director's independence of the writer that in Europe a talented director may start shooting with nothing to go on but a central idea or at best a skeletonized manuscript which serves as a miniature screenplay. The director may then encourage improvisation on the set by the actors, once he has explained the basic situation or circumstances of the scene in which they find themselves. Obviously, the writer who wishes to be considered an artist in films will have a much better chance if he not only writes his own screenplay but directs it as well. This is why a number of writers are becoming writer-directors.

"Collaboration" in screenwriting is a term that must be introduced. To most people, there is nothing untoward in two or more persons, working together on a project. But collaboration in Hollywood does not mean functioning in a joint fashion, except where a team of two or more writers start and finish the same screenplay. Collaboration means that after one writer has completed his version of a screenplay and been discharged from his duties, the entrepreneurs hire another writer to rewrite the first version, after which it is rewritten by still another writer and so on almost *ad infinitum*. It is this collaboration by compulsion that is most detested by screenwriters.

The industry's defense of this practice is that it has no

choice. Irving Thalberg, as quoted in *The Great Audience* by
Gilbert Seldes, has said:

*A Broadway producer with an investment of five hun-
dred dollars in a dramatic script, puts up another 500
and tells the author to work on his second act for another couple of months. I can't do that. I've got a schedule to meet. If a man brings in a script and it's got good
characters and dialogue but no comedy, I get a man who
can do comedy—and hope to God he won't spoil the
characters. Some people are weak on character-building,
and I put them to work with a man that's first-rate that
way. I know they don't like it, and I don't like it myself.
What can I do?*

Mr. Thalberg also said, "The writer is a necessary evil."

This kind of collaboration has resulted in an unfortunate
and self-defensive practice among the writers themselves.
Inasmuch as a writer's livelihood and reputation depend
upon the number of his screenplays which actually become
released motion pictures (many are abandoned at the
screenplay stage), a desperate or dishonest writer who is
assigned to revise a previous writer's screenplay often eliminates as much as he can of his predecessor's work, substituting a new version of his own. This "writing out" another
writer has to do with the system of credits by which a writer
is evaluated in the industry and is a reprehensible procedure
under any circumstances.

For the lucky screenwriter who survives collaboration
and gets a formal credit as the author of the final screenplay,
Hollywood has devised an additional travail. Having endured the mayhem of various studio executives while con-
structing his screenplay, the writer's services are dispensed
with when the script is about to undergo its most significant
transformation and be brought to life by actors and director.

This is the precise moment when the writer, familiar with every nuance of the script, immersed in the characters he has created, aware of the links and connections in the narrative, should be of enormous assistance—to prevent the careless and destructive rewriting that takes place on a set. But it is the rare producer or director who invites him to the shooting.

Perhaps the greatest ignominy the screenwriter endures is anonymity. From beginning to end, only his immediate superiors, a very limited circle, have any knowledge of his work. The dramatist and the television writer are sometimes included in anthologies, but rarely the man who writes for the screen. A small number of screenplays have achieved publication, but their circulation and readership are extremely limited. The well-turned sentence, the striking simile, the graceful metaphor are almost never seen or appreciated by the reading public. Here is a large group of professionals whose contributions have an international impact on ideas and cultural patterns, and who remain almost completely anonymous. For most of them, their closest approach to the world of letters is the shelf of leather-bound screenplays that graces their personal libraries, a pathetic attempt at simulated publication.

The lack of recognition remains one of the supremely aggravating aspects of screenwriting. A writer's name is flashed on the screen for approximately three and a half seconds. Of the two hundred million people who attend the movies weekly throughout the world, probably not more than one hundred nonprofessional members of the audience know the name of a single screenwriter.

The only public attention the writer receives is strictly parochial. The Screen Achievement Records Bulletin, issued by the Academy of Motion Picture Arts & Sciences, contains such one-line data as: "Jeremiah Jorgenson, joint story and screenplay, *The Fourteenth Apostle*, Columbia, 1951." This bulletin's circulation is limited to other writers, story editors and inquisitive producers. Annual awards are granted by the Writer's Guild to its members, and the Academy of Motion Picture Arts & Sciences presents a chosen few with the celebrated "Oscars," but these citations are often incestuous and do little to make the public aware that somebody must have written the words the actors speak. Outside the film industry, there are dozens of prizes for films, but none for film writers. The blackout is very nearly total. There is a review in the Academy files by a film critic who saw a presentation of Ann Sothern in a picture called *Maisie* and wrote, "Miss Sothern's unceasing flow of bright sayings redeems a dull script." Little more need be said.

There is another anomaly in the life of the screenwriter. Whereas the novelist or playwright can measure his success by the comments of critics and reviewers, the screenwriter's only testimonials are his "credits," the produced pictures he has written. These appear in a publication of the Writer's Guild of America, West. When a writer is "up" (being considered) for an assignment, the producer is able to estimate his talent by a rapid reference to his past record in this bulletin, which is kept up to date at all times.

A writer's credit is the *sine qua non* of his profession. Credit disagreements frequently arise when more than one writer has contributed to a screenplay, and these conflicts are settled by the writers themselves, through submission of the script in dispute to a board of fellow writers, unknown to each other and to the querying writer. The Writer's Guild of America, West, resolves more than one hundred and fifty such controversies each year. The relatively large number of arbitrations is not surprising; a credit is professional life or death to a writer.

Sometimes even adequate credits do not guarantee

entrée to a studio job. The producer may analyze his credits, but he is more likely to consider the financial success or failure of the writer's most recent picture. Yet no computer has been devised that can tell us which element determines the success of a picture. Was it the screenplay, the actors, the director, the producer, the publicity, the camera work, the subject matter, the basic book or play, or any combination of these? Where two or more names appear as authors, which one constructed the story, which the comedy dialogue, which the serious dialogue? How much of the final screenplay derived its inspiration from the five preceding screenplays?

Writers and bosses in Hollywood are natural enemies. From the very beginning of writing for films the screenwriter has inveighed against administrators who attempt to supervise the creative literary processes. Writers are convinced that Front Office dignitaries approach every screenplay with total recoil. Some of the finest unwritten invective in the English language has been applied to these officials, who are known to screenwriters as towers of jello and the abominable no-men. There is not much joy in Writer's Row when they recall the remark attributed to Eddie Mannix, when he was vice-president of Metro Goldwyn Mayer. Mannix called a story conference to discuss a writer's screenplay and invited the producer and the director to participate. When queried as to why the writer was not called upon to join the meeting, Mannix replied, "Writers clutter up a story conference."

One of the wittiest and most highly paid writers who ever came to Hollywood was Ben Hecht, whose antipathy for his employers was unbridled and unconcealed, but whose ability was so superior that even executives who smarted most from his blistering denunciations tried to hire him. A Hollywood executive is not burdened with sensitivity; he will cheerfully accept insults from anyone talented enough to provide him with what he wants—a picture that makes money. It was Hecht who inspired the now famous comment of an angry studio chief who said of him, "I never want to see that son-of-a-bitch on my lot again—unless I need him." No one in print has more accurately captured the atmosphere of a studio from the writer's viewpoint than Hecht. As unofficial spokesman for his fellow writers Hecht is at his best in "Enter, the Movies," included in Daniel Talbot's *Film: An Anthology:*

> *I have taken part in a thousand story conferences. I was always present as the writer. Others present were the "producer," the director and sometimes the head of the studio and a small tense group of his admirers. . . . The job of turning good writers into movie hacks is the producer's chief task. . . . I can recall a few bright ones among them, and fifty nitwits. The pain of having to collaborate with such dullards and to submit myself to their approvals was always acute. Years of experience failed to help. I never became reconciled to taking literary orders from them. I often prepared myself for a producer conference by swallowing two sleeping pills in advance. I have always considered that half of the large sum paid me for writing a movie script was in payment for listening to the producer and obeying him. I am not being facetious. The movies pay as much for obedience as for creative work. An able writer is paid a larger sum than a man of small talent. But he is paid this added money not to use his superior talents. I often won my battle with producers. I was able to convince them that their suggestions were too stale or too infantile. But I won such battles only as long as I remained on the grounds. The minute I left the studio my victory vanished. Every sour syllable of producer invention went*

*back into the script and every limping foot of it ap-
peared on the screen.*

Hecht's account is of another era, but it is as applicable to
the New Hollywood as to the Old.

Not all Hollywood writers are as dyspeptic as Ben
Hecht (or as gifted), nor do they all feel so strongly that
their art is being distorted, their integrity impugned, their
creativity aborted. On the contrary, many of them find in
Hollywood a way of life and work that is highly attractive in
many ways. The primary reason Hollywood writers do not
make good their mumbled threats to return to the writing of
novels or plays is—money. Hollywood still offers the possibility of more money than most writers ever attain. Though
there are only five screenwriters today among the approximately 3000 members of the Writers Guild of America, West,
who have long-term contracts (as opposed to 110 in 1947),
the returns are still impressive when compared to those
offered in the magazine and book worlds. It has been reliably
estimated that of the hundreds of thousands of freelance
writers working in America, only some four thousand earn a
living from their pens, a living that approximates $4500 a
year. Even with the present economic crisis facing the film
industry, the average annual sum earned by a Hollywood
writer is substantially more than that, and in good times his
income far surpasses that of all but a very few extremely popular fiction writers. While joblessness is endemic in Hollywood,
if and when a writer *does* secure a writing assignment for even
a relatively short time, his weekly pay is high enough to
carry him over the fallow periods.

During 1968, a total of $39,633,000 was paid to writers
employed in Hollywood by motion pictures and television
(most Hollywood writers now collect salaries from both
media). In 1969 the figure was $45,171,000; in 1970 it was
$41,710,000; the 1971 total was $43,100,000, and the esti-

mated figure for 1972 is close to $43,000,000. Writers will also receive approximately 15 percent of these totals, which will accrue from residuals—recompense from the sale to television of the pictures they have written plus the reruns of those written directly for TV. An honorable estimate of the average wage earned by a working writer in Hollywood would vary between $20,000 and $25,000 a year—considerably more than that earned by all but the most fortunate of today's freelance writers.

Not many, if any, Hollywood writers have dollar-sign-shaped swimming pools, Oxford educated butlers, and foreign cars equipped with telephones, but all in all, the lot of the Hollywood writer is by no means to be deplored when compared with that of writers in other fields.

It is important to remember that writers in Hollywood never write except for money. There is a stern clause in all writers' agreements that expressly forbids anything more speculative than an exchange of ideas across a conference table. Hollywood writers assume no financial risks; they do not gamble with their time and talent as a playwright or novelist does. Their scripts may be rejected ("shelved"), but this can only happen after they have been paid. "They ruin your stories," one writer has remarked. "They massacre your ideas. They prostitute your art. They trample on your pride. And what do you get for it? A fortune."

"The system under which writers work in Hollywood would sap the vitality of a Shakespeare. They are intelligent enough to know that they are writing trash, but they are not intelligent enough to do anything about it." That statement was made by Dalton Trumbo many years ago. Has there been a change in the New Hollywood? Will the Hollywood writer ever emerge from obscurity? Will he be able to stop writing "trash" and employ his talent for the creation of films with meaning and integrity? Will he ever see the day when his signature on a screenplay will matter to the public? Will he ever regard his own contribution to films with respect? Will he ever feel that his services are as his contract states, really "special, unique, unusual, extraordinary and of an intellectual character involving skill of the highest order"?

Only a very qualified "yes" can be given to these questions. Without a doubt certain barriers which impeded the writer in the past are being removed. Crude censorship has been replaced by total permissiveness. Adult themes formerly reserved for the stage or books can now be translated honorably onto the wider medium of the screen. An influx of mature foreign films has proven that the screen can be more than an opiate. The obligation to make films according to the formulas evolved by seven major studios is disappearing.

One obstacle, however, will continue to block the writer's ability to use his talents fully and honestly: Hollywood is an industry and an industry can only exist on profits; and until profits can come from something other than the sponsorship of mediocrity, the word "hack" will accurately describe most screenwriters. The Hollywood writer is a commercial contributor to a commercial enterprise, and it is only when that circumstance alters radically that the screenwriter in Hollywood will be ranked with the novelist or playwright as a creative personality. The current conglomerate owners will not become devotees of art—it has not happened during the past sixty years of the industry and there is no reason to think that it will happen in the future.

The screenwriter's profession has been described as making him feel "as though he were writing on sand with the wind blowing." But Hollywood is still an El Dorado, and it will always be one for the majority of writers who agree with Samuel Johnson that "no man but a blockhead ever wrote except for money."

A witty and true description of the Hollywood screenwriter is contained in a verse of Dorothy Parker's, "The Passionate Screenwriter To His Love," which appeared in *The*

Screen Writer and has been reprinted in Kenneth Mac-
Gowan's book *Behind the Screen.*

Oh, come, my love, and join with me
The oldest infant industry.
Come seek the bourne of palm and pearl,
The lovely land of Boy-Meets-Girl.
Come grace this lotus-laden shore,
This Isle of Do-What's-Done-Before.
Come, curb the new, and watch the old win,
Out where the streets are paved with Goldwyn.
Here let me guide your sedulous pen
To trace the proven lines again;
Here ply your quill, in glory dipt,
And see what happens to your script;
Hear how your phrases—metered, guarded,—
With actors' jokes are interlarded.
Oh, come, my love, nor fret the while
The mighty disregard your smile,
For Cohens, in this haughty small berg,
Bow but to God (Who's cut by Thalberg).
Oh, cast your scruples to the winds
And join us Pegasus' behinds!
Come, learn along with me, my sweet
How charming thrice a day to eat,
How good to bend the stubborn neck
And hail the rhythmic weekly cheque!
But when, my love, you have been here
A little less than half a year,
You start to talk, who once were dumb,
Of "what a wondrous medium,"
And "why, they haven't scratched the surface,"
(While grieved Mnemosyne hides her face)
And "here's the writer's noblest art"—
That day, my perjured love, we part!

THE PRODUCER

*I can never understand how anyone can take on the
responsibility for planning any big show without guidance
from God.*

As we have seen, producers did not exist in the formative
period of motion pictures. The director was king; such men
as David Wark Griffith, Mack Sennett, Frank Lloyd, James
Cruze were the film-makers of those early days. But as the
demand for films grew, the volume of pictures from individual studios became so great and so unmanageable that the
studio executives could not supervise the increased output
with only directors in charge. Lines of communication began
to be blurred. Thus, producers came into being. Their early
responsibilities were inconsequential; they operated largely
as administrative aides to the studio heads. Their duties were
mainly clerical, and as proof of their minimal importance,
such posts were ordinarily relgated to relatives or friends.
Experience and knowledge were not essential. In that respect
Hollywood has not changed drastically.

The producer has been compared to an orchestra conductor, a diplomat, a visionary, a general, an aesthetician, an impresario, an archbishop (honestly!), an entrepreneur, a taste-maker, an administrator and—yes, that too—a genius. But none of these descriptions originated in Hollywood, or if they did, they can be ascribed to ingenious press agents on the producer's payroll. In Hollywood, the producer is everyone's enemy. Only agents are subject to a greater amount of scorn. To those who like the producer least he is a lackey, a fool, a thief, a chameleon, a con man, and a Master of Instantaneous Indecision. He has also been described as "a man who asks a studio employee a question, gives him the answer, and tells him he's wrong"; or, as Martin Ragaway defines him in "A Hollywood Dictionary," "a clever man whose brain starts working the moment he gets up in the morning and doesn't stop until he gets to the studio."

The standard studio contract defines the services of a producer as follows: "Employers shall render all services customarily required of an individual producer of motion pictures in accordance with the customs and practices of the motion picture industry." The new producer reading his contract for clarification of these "customs and practices" will not be enlightened.

There is a second contractual clause concerning the producer's responsibilities which is equally nebulous but considerably more flattering: "The producer will also render such other services of an executive nature as may from time to time be assigned to him by the corporation commensurate with his knowledge, experience, talent and ability. . . ." This implies prior existence of "knowledge, experience, talent and ability" on the part of the producer, an optimistic assumption in the case of many contemporary producers who had never set foot on a studio lot before entering the profession, and whose only knowledge of motion pictures came from being members of the audience.

Let us see what lies behind the "knowledge, experience,

talent and ability" that are contractually demanded of a Hollywood producer. Let us determine, if we can, what his functions are. In essence, the producer is the supervisor of a film from start to finish, from the original idea or story to the completed picture. Inasmuch as cinema is admittedly the most complex and collaborative of all the arts, it is obvious that such a supervisor has weighty obligations. There are approximately one hundred and twenty-eight different crafts and skills called upon in the manufacture of a single picture, including a familiarity in depth with story, writing, directing, casting, editing, acting, wardrobe, cinematography, sound, film, color, dubbing, publicity, carpentry, architecture, set design, make-up, music, and lighting. It would be astonishing if any single executive had even a superficial knowledge of some of these highly specialized skills. Yet a producer is supposed to understand something about all of them, for it is he as commander-in-chief who must make the final decisions concerning every one of these numerous processes.

There have been producers in Hollywood who could cope with a considerable number of these diverse elements. These men were not da Vincis of the cinema, but they had the advantage of years of exposure to film-making. Few of the current crop of producers have come up from the ranks; few have had the requisite training, or know much, if anything, about the highly complex art of manufacturing films. Many a producer in the New Hollywood bears his title because he controlled a valuable "package," could provide his own financing, once functioned fleetingly as a television executive, or was a close friend or relative of the new corporate chiefs.

Whether it is because the new breed of inexperienced producers makes even their corporate employers insecure, or because Hollywood remains a land of paradox, it is instructive to know that no producers today are granted any real authority. They are putatively in charge of films which involve enormous sums of money, but in practice their so-called powers are severely confined. The restrictions are on two levels: there is a contractual limitation on their sovereignty, and there exists a group of technicians (the actual film-makers) who function whether or not there is a knowledgeable (or unknowledgeable) producer at the helm. In other words, the corporation heads exhibit very little faith in the producer's alleged ability or competence, though theoretically they have hired him for these very qualities.

The standard producer contract contains a revealing protective (for the studio) clause:

> *It is expressly understood and agreed that the story, budget, director and cast of each photoplay produced hereunder and all other creative and artistic controls and business decisions shall be vested in the corporation. . . . The corporation shall also have the right to designate a supervisor or executive producer to work with the producer. . . . The producer will render services conscientiously and to the full limit of the producer's ability and as instructed by the corporation in all matters, including those involving artistic taste and judgement.* (Underscoring mine.)

This corporate mandate applies with equal force to the so-called independent producer, whose role in Hollywood will be discussed later.

These restraints on the producer not only strike at the core of his job, they expose several of the more bizarre aspects of the New Hollywood. "Story, budget, director, cast, creative, business, taste, judgment"—everything that goes into the construction of a film is vested in the corporation.

What else is there? The producer ends by being in complete charge of a film over which he has no real authority. By making each of these decisions subject to the corporate will of the studio, the producer, supposedly in charge of his picture, is relegated to the role of a subordinate.

Is it possible that the studio executives know what they are doing? Judging by this contract provision, the answer is yes. Another question arises: If so, why did they engage these men in the first place? To that there is no satisfactory answer. One can only surmise that there is a need for some sort of supervision and stewardship—as distinct from decision-making—and that a so-called producer is as effective as any other official in that capacity.

A further point the contract terms betray is that the producer may indeed turn out to be the flunkey his detractors label him, in spite of his determination not to be. How else could he hold his job? Since any decisions he reaches can be legally countermanded by the corporation employing him, he remains a highly paid functionary with an impressive title and little else.

If we single out a few of the components cited in the producer's contract, especially those creative elements "involving artistic taste and judgment," we can better appreciate not only the producer's limitations but why the corporation restricts him in so many ways. For example, to be able to select a story for filming from among the over twenty-five thousand books published annually in America alone is no mean feat. That by itself—assuming the producer had time for thoughtful and measured consideration—would demand a highly literate and discriminating mind with a sensitivity for the spoken as well as the written word. Few producers qualify in that respect. To be able to guide a screenwriter around dangerous shoals is to possess the temperament and talent of a writer oneself. Few producers are so endowed. In respect to the direction of a film, any producer who endeavors to "aid" his director invites a feud on the set. To cast a picture correctly is an art of its own. To select and supervise the cameraman, to consult intelligently with the set designer, to oversee the work of the cutter—all require great skill and knowledge.

Nor do the duties mentioned above take into account those of a business nature, such as conferences with the comptroller on the budget, constant surveillance of the shooting schedule, and the negotiation of numerous contracts and agreements. Here, too, special expertise is needed. And thus we might go on down a long list. It is this lack of professional knowledge in an industry that requires it that makes artisans tremble when a producer offers guidance in their fields, and has given rise to the cry of anguish addressed to most producers: "Please don't help me—to fail!"

It has been said that the studio protects itself against its own producers by limiting their authority, and by employing a number of technicians, specialists in the various crafts utilized in the making of films. These are known loosely as the "back-lot crew." It is they who solve seemingly insoluble problems and perform miracles of design, invention, construction, editing, and carpentry. These men, the sound engineers, film editors, laboratory workers, dubbing crew, assistant directors, unit managers, gaffers, grips, location personnel, art designers, set constructors—the list is as long as it is impressive—are the real workers of Hollywood. Their creativity and ingenuity serve as a built-in protection against perfunctory or incompetent producer supervision. No film could exist without them. Highly qualified, trained, inventive, these men have often spent decades refining their particular skills. They know instantly whether or not their producer knows what he is talking about, and they compensate for any ignorance he reveals.

All studios, no matter how decimated they may now be as a result of conglomerate policies, continue to maintain such a staff of specialists. Even if the studio is not at work on its own productions, the services of these experts provide a lure to outside producers who wish to rent studio space and facilities. Their departments are usually headed by a man who has worked for years in the lower levels of his specialized occupation. Only a stubborn producer does not pay heed to these talented subordinates who help make "his" picture. It is this cabinet of advisors who, together with the director, produce the picture; they are responsible for it in a hundred different ways. The incalculable importance of these men and women should be recognized and due homage accorded them. So valuable are they that from time to time proposals have been entertained of eliminating the producer both nominally and actually and having his screen credit replaced by a more truthful one stating that the film was produced by the studio—that is, by the back-lot crew and the director. However, the producer syndrome is too entrenched to envision such a change in the foreseeable future.

Unless he is exceptionally gifted, the producer has only administrative and bureaucratic duties. To sit in a music recording session with a typical producer who knows nothing about either sound or music is an agonizing experience. To attend a story conference where the producer is incapable of contributing a single idea of merit is traumatic for the screenwriter. To watch a producer advise a cameraman or order a make-up adjustment is painful.

There is no training course for a producer; the universities and colleges have no classes in producership. There is no test to pass; there are no rules to master. Consequently, rank amateurism is no bar to achieving producer status. Producers come from anywhere and everywhere. Broadway has provided some recruits, but there is a considerable difference between producing a New York play and undertaking a motion picture costing millions of dollars and involving the services of hundreds of people. It is widely accepted that "any guy" can become a producer, just as "anyone" can be an agent. The judgment that comes through trial and error is not essential; professionalism may be desired but is not required.

Since "any guy" can become a producer and the financial rewards are attractive, various members of the film industry have tried to enter the producer fraternity, among them actors. For years actors have complained about producers, their inability to appreciate the artistry of the performer, their miscastings, their forcing of players into stereotyped roles, and most of all their garnering of huge revenues solely on the strength of the players' box-office standing. At least so the actors believed. Consequently, when the studio power-structures began to crumble and actors suddenly found themselves no longer "saddled" with long-term contracts, they seized the opportunity to form their own companies, to produce their own pictures, and to reap the profits for themselves.

Of course, not all these actors were motivated by money alone. Certain actors felt, and they were right, that too many producers lacked the courage or interest to film subjects of a political, social, or artistic nature that might be deemed controversial or a challenge to the Establishment. In any event, whether persuaded by cupidity, jealousy, aesthetic or social convictions, a number of actors became producers. The results have not been inspiring, either because their personal vanity made it impossible for them to subordinate themselves to the picture as a whole, or because they could not master the economics of the business. At one time producer-actor companies flourished with such people as Clint Eastwood, Kirk Douglas, John Wayne, and Jack Lemmon as their owners, but most of these have collapsed; the few that have survived are merely corporate shells which sell the services of the actors to studios and independent producers.

Gregory Peck, one of the actors turned producer, expresses his opinion of this in Charles Hamblett's *The Hollywood Cage*:

> *For years we actors have been fighting for our so-called artistic freedom. We wanted to be rid of the moguls and accountants. We damned the studio for their materialism and lack of taste. Now, most of us are on our own. So what happens? This morning I had to call my office and scrap a production on which people have been working for months. Thousands of dollars were invested, but I decided it would be best to chuck it now rather than risk making a bad picture and losing more money. . . . I tell you there are times when I wish Hollywood actors had retained the status of bums and gypsies and left the planning to others. Right now, I'm tempted to say the hell with all of it. In effect, I have complete control over everything I do. A year or two back, this was considered to be some kind of a victory of Art over Tyranny. Now I'm not so sure.*

The forays of actors into production have not resulted in major contributions to the advancement of the industry. Neither the studios nor the actors—nor the public—have derived any signal benefits. Few of their films initiated any revolutionary departures from the staple product manufactured by the professional producers, and few of them have been commercially successful. Perhaps Samuel Goldwyn was right when he said, "Let actors act, directors direct, and producers produce."

Still other aspirants for producership are the screenwriters. But unlike the agents and some of the actors, they are not relinquishing their former profession. They have become a hyphenated phenomenon, the writer-producer. Over the years writers have complained that producers ride rough-shod over their screenplays and that a writer who sees a filmed version of his manuscript just as he wrote it is, indeed, an exception. Suffice it to say, one of the ways a writer can partially protect his cherished screenplay is to produce it himself. (Of course the only complete protection is to direct it too.) Consequently, writer-producers such as Paul Monash, Stirling Silliphant, David Karp, Richard Alan Simmons are coming into prominence in Hollywood. Thus far their incursion has not been a notable one (in Europe it is much more evident), but the emergence of screenwriters as producers should be salutary for the industry, for the writer has a sensitivity and an imagination that the average producer does not possess.

Before turning to the so-called independent producer, it is well to recall that independent producers existed before the decline of Hollywood's monopolistic studio system and the advent of the conglomerates. There were not many and they left little imprint on the industry, but there were two giants among them, two men whose courage and artistry contributed memorably to the history of the motion picture. These two were David O. Selznick and Samuel Goldwyn. They gave the word "producer" and the word "independent" authority and significance. Almost all of their productions were made during Hollywood's Golden Period and bore the hallmarks of taste and distinction. When applied to them the phrase "independent producer" had a meaning it does not have in the New Hollywood where it is used much more loosely.

Today practically every producer in Hollywood is an independent producer; the classification has become all-embracing. Staff or salaried producers are hard to find in the New Hollywood. Ex-actor, ex-agent, one-time writer, friend, relative—they are all independents. It has been estimated that independents packaged and produced over eighty-five percent of all the movies made in America in 1970, a percentage which can only increase as contract personnel are further eliminated by the conglomerates.

The differences between a salaried producer of the Old Hollywood and an independent producer of the New Hollywood are not great. As a matter of fact, a fair number of the now independent producers are the same men who func-- tioned previously as salaried employees before they were discharged. Unless he is wholly independent, with his financing coming from personal resources, the independent producer is subject to the same editorial and creative proscriptions he experienced while under salary. If his financing comes from a bank, he still needs studio approval of his project, for no bank will sponsor an independent film until assured of its release through a major studio. And as a final comment on his "independence," he signs precisely the same standard contract that he did in his earlier incarnation. The one difference is that his new independence permits him to participate in the profits, if there are any.

In her book *The Contemporary Cinema*, Penelope Houston describes the Hollywood independent producer:

This opening of the door to independent production provided, in theory, opportunities for risk and adventure; and proved, when it came to the point, that producers, directors, and actors, left to themselves, would make much the same kind of films that they had been working on for their studio overlords. And independence, of course, is a word subject to infinite qualification. The producer still has to come to terms with his financial backers and with distributors; he has to deal with agents, with their philosophy of the "package deal," whereby to acquire the particular script he wants he may have to take a director or a star along with it; he has to manipulate all the complex human factors that go into the making of a film. If he lacks the burden of studio overheads, he also cannot afford the luxury of making commercial blunders, confident that whatever happens there will still be a studio behind him. If he operates cheaply, he knows that the sensational subject will be the quickest seller; if he works on the big scale, he competes for the latest best-sellers along with the studios. He knows that bankers more readily advance finance if a big star name is attached to a picture; and the stars, freed from the long-term contracts holding them to a particular studio, demand their sizeable cut of the profits. Actors and directors roam from one assignment to the next, from one studio to another. Power shifts from the studio bosses, the paternal despots who used to control their careers, to the agents who negotiated their contracts.

In short, even if an independent is able to make a film entirely in accord with his own dictates, desires, and money he must still come to a major studio—completed film and hat in hand—for its marketing and distribution. There are a quantity of self-financed films either languishing in rented film vaults or being shown sporadically in various sections of the country for short runs, films which have been rejected by the large companies for release. (Incidentally, the studios themselves have accumulated an impressive number of unreleased, abandoned productions at a total cost estimated at well over $50 million.) The major companies no longer own chains of theaters; this monopoly was outlawed many years ago; but they do maintain expert and efficient sales organizations throughout the world, offices for the selling, release, and distribution of films without which few motion pictures would ever reach any sizeable circulation. These sales and distribution organizations are powerful, and any film-maker who does not use them is ensuring that his picture will not be viewed by many people. Efforts are being made to establish new releasing-distribution companies to offset this commercial stranglehold, but as of today the old-line studio corporations still remain in control. It is very expensive to inaugurate and maintain distribution organizations with offices and personnel all over the world, and in these trying economic times it is more difficult than ever. The cost of opening a single movie in New York City ranges between $30,000 and $80,000 for the theater rental and the promotional campaign, and a national release could involve as much as $500,000.

One minor difference between the independent producer and his salaried predecessor is that not having studio financing, the independent producer must purchase his story or property with his own funds, which are supposed to be refunded by the studio when it acquires the property from him as part of a package. This is known as "front" or "development" money. This might appear to be a serious obstacle, but film writers have accommodated themselves to the change. They are perfectly aware that most independent producers cannot pay the large sums the studios could. Hence, a *modus operandi* has been devised whereby the independent producer acquires an option on the property for a small sum together with a stipulation guaranteeing the author additional money out of profit participation. The independent producer operates along similar lines with actors, directors, and screenwriters. He thus pays only a fraction of the artist's established fee or what has come to be called his "eating money," and this enables the producer to keep his initial costs to a minimum. This form of speculation by the author, star, screenwriter, and director on a profit-sharing basis is sometimes referred to as "if" money: it will only become real money if and when the package is sold and if and when the picture makes a profit. The procedure is novel inasmuch as the studios—unless forced to do so by artists of commanding box-office stature—are congenitally averse to giving away any profits, even of an "if" variety.

Any summary of the differences between the independent producer and the salaried producer would focus on money and security. The Old Hollywood producer was usually under contract for long periods of time. Barring a display of shattering ineptitude, he stayed on salary even if one or more of his projects was abandoned at the writing stage; and he could count on his picture being distributed once it reached the shooting phase. In the New Hollywood, an independent producer's stay at a studio is usually limited to the company's approval of one project at a time; he must finance the story purchase and often the writing of the screenplay himself; he must develop the required package ingredients for his film without the power of a studio to support him; most important of all, he must operate as a super-salesman to sell his services and his package to the studio before his picture can be produced. So we see that even the independent producer basically depends on the studio system.

In general, there isn't much difference between Old Hollywood films and New Hollywood films, which adhere in the main to conventional box-office formulae. There is one exception, however, though it may be only a passing phase. Some of today's independent producers have become involved in a new kind of film—new, that is, in that it was formerly shown surreptitiously in private clubs rather than in neighborhood theaters. Taking commercial advantage of an era of permissiveness, they have concentrated on the shock-cinema, pictures filled with sexuality in the most extreme and graphic terms. These films are for the most part contemporary variants of earlier "stag" or "nudie" films. This erotica is proliferating so rapidly that it is fast becoming imitative and cliché, as standardized and stereotyped as the slick, glossy pictures that preceded it in the days of strict censorship. Because these films are carbon copies of each other, they have already become commonplace and banal, and their audience appeal is markedly declining. The novelty is wearing thin. The copulation explosion on the screen is subsiding.

Clearly independence does not equal art, at least not in Hollywood. Indubitably, there are some independent producers who are making conscientious efforts to avoid the commonplace, but there are not many, and when one does initiate a project of taste and integrity it is often mutilated by the sponsoring studio, if not rejected outright at its inception. For the releasing studios are interested in profit, not art; profit, not prestige; profit, not quality. A certain number of films that are distinguished, authentic productions of discernment and imagination do come out of the New Hollywood, but as any historian of films would be quick to point out, approximately the same number of good pictures were produced by the Old Hollywood. The Old Hollywood was not an enemy of good films; all it asked was that the "good" films return a profit. But the percentage was not high then and it is not high now. Hollywood is convinced that mediocrity is safest in the long run; that profits come from the undiscriminating, not the discriminating. An independent producer soon loses his independence—and his producer status—if his film fails. One who has not failed is Ross Hunter: "I don't want to hold a mirror up to life as it is. I just want to show the part which is attractive—not freckled faces and broken teeth, but smooth faces and pearly white teeth." Mr. Hunter's philosophy is symptomatic of a large number of the New Hollywood producers.

Although the art critic Erwin Panofsky has said that

"The commercial producer can both educate and pervert the public," the majority of Hollywood producers are not primarily or even secondarily interested in doing either. Even if they were, the commercial world in which they move would render such ambitions difficult, if not impossible, to realize. Expediency, compromise, accommodation, adjustment, conciliation—these are important words in the producer's lexicon. During the making of a film there is steady pressure on the producer to please anyone and everyone—the stars, the financiers, and executives, the director, the studio owners, the publicists, the salesmen. As a result he sometimes loses sight of his original intention. The producer is badgered on every side by people whose knowledge of audience receptivity is no greater than his, but who frequently have the power to enforce their conjectures and surmises. Not that the producer knows what the public wants, but at least in the initial phases of his project he might have known what *he* wanted. The chances of his vision coming to fruition are miniscule, however. Unless he is using his own funds and can afford to defy the major studios because his product is so appealing they will sponsor its distribution on *his* terms, he can never subscribe to Samuel Goldwyn's dictum, "I make my pictures to please myself." Mr. Goldwyn was able to say this because he was self-financed at all times.

Assuredly one of the ways for a Hollywood producer to invite failure is to believe in the cinema as an art form. If a producer has an artistic conscience and abhors *kitsch*, he will find Hollywood unreceptive. David O. Selznick put it bluntly: "If you are primarily concerned with something that is usually called personal artistic integrity, you don't belong in the business of making commercial pictures." Despite all the talk about the new freedom of the artist in films, the American producer is still the victim and the follower of the system that began sixty years ago.

The latest producer-recruits—the agents—are businessmen, and this development may well be a direct reflection of the new owners' point of view, which is predominantly along fiscal lines. That, at least, is the opinion of Robert Kaufman, one of the new breed of writers, who said in the March 13, 1970, issue of *Entertainment World*, "Today's producers are mostly organizers—but organizers in the business and financial sense, *not in the creative sense*" (italics mine). It is a fact that most of the new wave of producers who entered Hollywood in the wake of the conglomerates are "organizers in the business and financial sense." Unfortunately, while ability in business may be an art of its own, it does not equate with the ability to make good motion pictures.

Ben Hecht, whose description of the Hollywood writer was quoted earlier, has also described the Hollywood producer. In Daniel Talbot's *Film: An Anthology*, Hecht writes:

The producer's place in movie-making is a matter that, in Hollywood, has not yet been cleared up. I shall try to bring some clarity to it. The big factory where movies are made is run by a super-producer called Head of the Studio who sits in the Front Office and is as difficult of access as the Grand Lama. He is the boss, appointed by the studio Owner himself. Thus, despite the veneration in which he is held by the thousand studio underlings, he is actually the greatest of the movieland stooges. He must bend his entire spirit to the philosophy of the movie Owner—"make money." He must translate this greedy cry of the Owner into a program for his studio. He must examine every idea, plot or venture submitted to him from the single point of view of whether it is trite enough to appeal to the masses. His immediate underlings are the producers. He has hired them to do the actual movie making for him . . . men who will keep their heads in the noisy presence of writers and directors and not be car-

ried away by art in any of its subversive guises. There are different kinds of producers in the studios, ranging from out-and-out illiterates to philosophers and aesthetes. But all of them have the same function. Their task is to guard against the unusual. They are the trusted loyalists of cliché. Writers and directors can be carried away by a "strange" characterization or a new point of view; a producer, never. . . . I discovered early in my movie work that a movie is never any better than the stupidest man connected with it. There are times when this distinction may be given to the writer or director. Most often it belongs to the producer.

Though efforts have been made to dislodge producers from their uneasy chairs, they will remain one of Hollywood's permanent fixtures, serving as business buffers between the Front Office and those writers, directors, and even occasionally actors who endeavor to inject art into what is an ailing business. The use of producers in such a capacity may be a belated recognition of their only true function in the Hollywood film factories.

THE FUTURE

If all the serious lyric poets, composers, painters and sculptors were forced by law to stop their activities, a rather small fraction of the general public would become aware of the fact and a still smaller fraction would seriously regret it. If the same thing were to happen with the movies the social consequences would be catastrophic.

ERWIN PANOFSKY

At this critical moment in cinematic history, with Hollywood bedeviled by changes, floundering and bewildered, it may seem foolhardy to speculate about its future. Nevertheless, it might prove rewarding to indulge in some few surmises on its destiny under the guidance of the conglomerates.

Let us start by turning time backward to an article by D. W. Griffith published in *Colliers* of May 3, 1924, and reprinted in Harry M. Geduld's book *Film Makers on Film Making*. Mr. Griffith made some remarkable predictions about "The Movies 100 Years From Now." He foretold the emergence of the wide screen; he foresaw that "colour photography would be perfected and made practical"; that "airplane passenger lines would operate motion pictures"; that

144

homes would have "private projection rooms"; and that many "subjects in our schools would be taught largely with the use of picture play and the educational animated picture." He forewarned his readers that by the year 2024 "it would cost perhaps twice as much as it costs today to see the really first-class cinema."

Only two of his prophecies have not been fulfilled: one stemmed from a violent prejudice, and the other from a naive faith in mankind. Griffith's dislike, amounting to hatred, of what he labeled "our so-called speaking pictures," led him to assume that any attempts to use sound to further speech in films would be disastrous. "We do not want now," he wrote, "and we never shall want the human voice with our films. . . . Music—fine music—will always be the voice of the silent drama. There is no voice in the world like the voice of music." This was his one error in evaluating the technical progress of films.

His second mistake derived from his conviction that the transcendent communication values of motion pictures would abolish war, "eliminating from the face of the civilized world all armed conflict. . . . With the use of the universal language of pictures the brotherhood of man will have been established throughout the earth." Would that he had been right!

One of his less philosophic forecasts has already come true, that in the years to come "there would be no concentrated production such as our Hollywood of to-day," and that films would be manufactured all over the globe. To the conglomerates confronted with the current hegira from Hollywood, Griffith's accuracy as a soothsayer must seem as prescient as it is depressing.

But let us move on from Griffith and his prophecies in 1924 to the reality of Hollywood in the '70s. Let us examine Hollywood today in terms of tomorrow. From an industrial viewpoint, its immediate future is charged with innovations, rich with possibilities for economic benefit. Unfortunately, they do not offer any panacea for Hollywood's chronic ailments, but they will be welcomed enthusiastically in this period of declining revenues.

It has been said that Hollywood needs "regular miracles" to stay alive. Thus far, they have come to pass with requisite frequency. Sound was introduced at a time when the industry was foundering. The invention and perfection of color was a life-saving contribution during a period of shrinking box-office receipts; and the wide screen helped at another low point. Again and again Hollywood has seen its customer appeal diminish, its powers fade, only to be rescued by a "regular miracle." These miracles were invariably of a mechanical nature, the products of brilliant technicians, and they were always transitory—the economic comfort they brought never had an enduring effect. It would appear that Hollywood is in constant need of assistance from some outside force.

Once again a mechanical marvel is about to come to the rescue—this time from the realm of electronics. This particular miracle is the cassette, which means casket or money-box (which it may well become), defined in cinematic terms by Webster as a "light-tight machine for holding films or plates for use in a camera." A cassette as used in motion pictures is a small plastic box containing spools of tape or film in which images as well as sounds have been stored and which when combined with a playback device attached to a television receiving set will put any program of the spectator's choice on his living room screen.

Numerous enterprising organizations have already seized upon the potential advantages of the cassette or video cartridge, and it is very much a reality, though still in its early stages of manufacture. A variety of rival firms such as RCA, CBS, Sony, Ampex, Westinghouse, Brunswick, Motorola, Avco, Telefunken, Philips-Norelco, and other smaller companies are in active production of these items. The one perfected by CBS seems to be in the vanguard at the moment. This is a system called The Electric Video Recording, known in film circles by its acronymic name of EVR. The EVR is made of plastic about one-sixth of an inch thick and can hold 750 feet of film.

These machines are currently very expensive, with prices even higher than those on television sets when they were first made available for public purchase. But it is obvious that their cost will ultimately be scaled down to a point where they will be accessible at modest prices. To buy an EVR today, together with its player instrument and some 30 hours of film entertainment, would cost the consumer close to $5000. There are, however, over 60,000,000 television sets in America, all of which could be equipped with the cassette-plus-playback system. By catering to this vast aggregation of viewers the manufacturer could eventually lower the cost per unit to a figure at which every television owner could afford to have such an attachment.

There is another, somewhat different, system of reproducing films on television sets called "holograms" or the recording of images "holographically," which is a form of "lenseless photography." This involves the use of laser beams and thus far demands extreme care when used, since uncontrolled manipulation of laser beams can injure human beings. However, if this device can be perfected it would be even cheaper than the cassette, and in addition it would offer the possibility of achieving a three-dimensional effect.

The major studios in Hollywood are eagerly anticipating the advent of the cassette, for the immediate revenue it promises would seem to be extraordinary. Twentieth Century Fox has already given CBS the right to transpose all of its catalogue of films into cassette form, only reserving its most recent productions for theatrical showings. Other studios are studying this new development but are waiting until they can determine which process of reproduction will be most effective and most popular.

In addition to the money to be derived from the sale of their own entertainment films, the studios will also be able to service other business organizations which will use cassettes. Large corporations such as IBM have already announced that they will put all their instruction films for employees and customers into cassettes and will probably turn to film companies to perform this task for them, at least until they can install their own picture-making subsidiaries. The highly film-conscious worlds of education, both public and private, are busy preparing curricula in which illustrated lectures will be given by cassettes, and they are considering the transfer of textbooks into these same cartridges, since a multi-volume encyclopaedia can be transcribed onto a single such cassette. Until these educational institutions can develop their personal film-producing departments, the major motion picture companies will be called upon to manufacture and supply the films.

Naturally, Hollywood is rejoicing in these developments. In an interview in *Variety* of August 9, 1970, Joseph Levine, president of Embassy Films, one of America's largest independent companies stated: "I predict that within five years you will be able to make a ten million dollar film and get all your money back in one night. There will be 25 million homes with cable TV or cassettes."

Cassettes will unquestionably benefit the beleaguered film industry, but paradoxically they carry with them a serious threat to the *status quo*. On the one hand, Hollywood film-makers will for some few years be the only ones capable of providing new material to meet the demands cassettes will initiate. Moreover, Hollywood will be able to rent or sell all of its old pictures in cassette form, at least until their copyrights expire—copyrights which are valid for fifty-six years in most instances. For the cassette owner, these new inventions will be superior to films now being shown on televison in that they will not be interrupted by commercials; they can be seen at a time convenient to the viewer and as often as he wishes; and the image projected will be much larger than the one on current television sets, since the manufacturers envision the eventual installation of wall-sized screens. In addition, he will have the great advantage of choosing his own films.

The deleterious side-effect of this, of course, is that cassettes in private homes will erode even further attendance at neighborhood theaters. Thus what may be the source of welcome revenue for a period of time will concomitantly exercise a depressing effect on the average motion picture theater income which is now Hollywood's principal resource. Whether cassette revenue will compensate for the loss, or whether cassettes themselves will become obsolescent and be replaced by some other mechanical marvel, are unanswerable questions. But Hollywood, living as it always has in the present, is not overly concerned with the future. To solve the current economic crisis is all that matters; after all, tomorrow is another day.

Apart from the cassettes, there will also be a change in the theater complex that dots America. This is already in progress, the creation and establishment of what are called mini-theaters of three hundred to four hundred seats. These small theaters, similar to the "art houses" in large cities, can be administered on a very economical basis since they can be supervised by a staff of two people, one of whom will operate the projection machine while the other sells the tickets—and the popcorn. Paralleling the growth of such mini-theaters will be the conversion to other uses or the razing of many of the large movie palaces which have been plagued with empty seats.

On the distant horizon for Hollywood is a reduction in

the quantity of very expensive films, for it has been found that the financial risks of such ventures are far too great. These multi-million-dollar productions will by no means be totally abandoned, however. Always irresolute, Hollywood will undertake a number of high-budget pictures despite denials to the contrary. It cannot resist buying best-selling novels and smash-hit plays, and inasmuch as the prices for these are extremely high and going higher, Hollywood will "protect" its huge investment in stories by backing them with costly casts, mountings, and advertising. We will still see some "blockbusters," as they are called in film trade jargon, though not as many as before.

The New Hollywood will devote some of its energies and facilities to the marketing of eight- and sixteen-milli-meter versions of its films to cinema clubs, film societies, and private individuals, customer groups which are growing rapidly. Previously, such sales have been made by outside organizations, not connected with the major studios, but this market is now of sufficient consequence to warrant the elimi-nation of such middlemen distributors.

Up to now we have explored Hollywood's future on the business and technical level, but what lies in the offing for the men who make the pictures? What do the years ahead hold for The Agent, The Director, The Star, The Writer, and The Producer?

First, The Agent. He will continue to dominate the in-dustry just as he does today; in fact, it is not unlikely that his control will become even greater. The unprofessionalism of the new conglomerate proprietors will tend to make them lean more heavily on those alert, omnipresent agents who smilingly ease corporate burdens by offering ready-made packages. The smaller agencies will vanish or become satel-lites of the major agencies.

Second, The Director. Here the lines of the future are

clearly marked, for the director is rapidly emerging as the most important creative contributor to films, especially when allied with a superior screenwriter. Whereas today the star is still the essential ingredient of a film package for securing financial support or distribution, the day will come when the director will have equal weight. This trend will become more evident when the director is either a writer-director or a director-producer, or essays the triple combination of writer-director-producer, consolidations that will occur more frequently. More and more respect is being given the director. Audiences throughout the world are becoming familiar with the names and achievements of individual directors; film festivals devoted to their work are becoming commonplace; film heads are relying more and more upon the director's accomplishments. It is entirely possible that the director will again become the king of films, able to dictate his own terms to the studio conglomerate that hires him.

Third, The Star. He or she will blaze brighter than ever, whether the audience is sitting at home with cassettes or lined up in front of a theater. The star system will never be eclipsed, only the names and the faces will change.

Fourth, The Writer. The writer will grow in importance, and his key contribution to the art of the motion picture will win the recognition it deserves. He will be welcomed rather than tolerated. More and more writers will devote their talents to the screen from the very beginning, rather than after having been seduced, willingly or not, from other kinds of writing. Furthermore, there will be a change in Hollywood's attitude toward those writers emerging from film courses in colleges which now have curricula for cinematic arts. The demand for films to feed millions of cassettes will require the services of many more writers than now work in Hollywood, and the industry will be forced to cherish them, at least until cassettes are replaced by something else. From the negative side, one of the reasons more writers will adopt screenwriting as a means to a literary livelihood will be the demise of many of their former markets such as newspapers and magazines.

Fifth, The Producer. Producers will continue to exist, but the title will be nominal. As the director undertakes more and more responsibility, the producer's functions will decrease. Where a producer is retained as an individual in charge of a film, his actual operation will be restricted to that of coordinator, administrator, comptroller, negotiator, and business watchdog for the conglomerate. The category of independent producer will continue to expand, and these men will be chosen largely for their ability to develop, organize, and present a package to the studio for filming, not for any signal creative capacities. Business-oriented specialists will become producers, men whose expertise lies almost wholly in finance and who know little or nothing of showmanship or entertainment values. No illusion of their alleged artistic acumen will remain.

The future will include more and more filming outside of Hollywood, chiefly in Europe. As a result, there will be sporadic and costly surveys made by the major companies of possible amalgamation into one mammoth studio complex which would permit the sharing of costs and facilities by all companies. One or two such consolidations may even be attempted (Columbia and Warners are now exploring the prospect), but the odds are against the entire industry using a single area for all its productions. As Thomas Pryor, editor of *Variety*, said in one of his articles on this subject, "It's just too practical an idea to be implemented." Failing such mergers, and until cassettes prove to be the bonanza they promise, the studios will continue to rent their empty stages to independent television producers, while at the same time developing their own television programs to market to the networks. More and more of the real estate assets owned by the studios will be sold for needed capital. Studios will make extensive investments in other leisure-time ventures having nothing to do with films—such as resort hotels and vacation cruise ships. Those conglomerates now in command of Hollywood will probably be supplanted by others as the initial owners weary of the problems attendant on their expensive playthings, but Hollywood will never return to its former condition of studios controlled and run by individuals. The conglomerates are here to stay.

What about art and aesthetics? Does the present contain any sign that the future Hollywood will raise its standards so that films of quality and distinction will be manufactured? Will films fulfill their potential as not only diverting entertainment but also achievements that might raise the cultural level of American society as a whole?

So long as Hollywood is an integral part of the private enterprise system, to which it is now more firmly than ever attached, *and so long as art in films is not demanded or required or even requested by the majority of movie-goers*, art will find acceptance in films only when it is profitable. Art has never been an appreciated commodity in the boardrooms of Hollywood, nor does the future promise a change in this attitude. The motion picture industry "is a business that can work, if it's run like a business rather than as an art form," said James Aubrey, newly appointed president of Metro Goldwyn Mayer, in *Variety* of November 10, 1971.

The new Establishment that controls Hollywood is the old Establishment under another name, and when Jack Valenti said in *Variety* of April 16, 1971, that there is "no longer a film establishment," he was ignoring reality. There is an establishment, the establishment of the conglomerates. Nor is Mr. Valenti any more correct in saying that nowadays "creative people more often than not are in command." All distribution and decision-making power is in the hands of the conglomerates, and the word "independent" when applied to a producer is nothing but a genuflective misnomer.

Hollywood will not become a citadel of art as long as audiences indicate their preference for the commonplace, and barring a miraculous change in our entire culture complex, such an alternative does not seem to be in the offing. Dwight Macdonald, in an article in *Mass Culture: The Popular Arts in America* (edited by Bernard Rosenberg and David Manning White), observes that "There seems to be a Gresham's law in cultural as well as monetary circulation: bad stuff drives out the good, since it is more easily understood and enjoyed. Good art competes with *kitsch*, serious ideas compete with commercialized formulae—and the advantage lies all on one side."

Is the future for films of artistry and integrity then as bleak as it has been in the past? Would it be impossible within the framework of Hollywood as it is now constituted to encourage some few experimental films that attempt a high level of artistry, at least as a part of the total film output? Can we visualize a Hollywood in which profit would be honored, yet would allow a percentage of that profit to back films which might justify its claim to being what has been called the most important new art form of the twentieth century?

For many years the U.S. government did nothing to provide aid for the performing arts such as music, ballet, theater, poetry, and films. That was left to the states and cities, and, more frequently, to private beneficence. In 1965 a milestone was reached with the establishment of the National Foundation on the Arts and the Humanities. For the first time appropriations were to be given to foster modern dance companies, major and metropolitan orchestras, opera companies, choral institutions, and jazz programs, and also to include grants to creative artists in music, drama, literature, films, architecture, and the folk arts. Congress voted a fund of $40 million in fiscal

1971, to be divided between the arts and the humanities. Subsequently, this figure was whittled down to allotments of some $13 million for the humanities and approximately $15 million for the arts. For fiscal 1972 the arts were granted $29,750,-000. Using the latter figure as a basis for comment, that means the American government contributes approximately 15 cents per person to further the arts. Let us look at other countries whose gross national product and per capita incomes are far below that of the United States. Austria, with a population of 7 million people, disburses $2.00 per person; Canada, with a population of 20 million people, spends $1.40 per person. West Germany contributes $2.42; Sweden, $2.00; Israel, $1.34; Britain, $1.33.

It is not that the United States government is against subsidization. It subsidizes the American farmer to the tune of $3.5 billion a year. The maritime industry receives about $500 million every year. Airlines are benefited by approximately $100 million; oil and other mineral industries, thanks to depletion allowances (an indirect subsidy), by some $1.3 billion. The bill for federal help in home ownership, which is subsidized by deduction for interest, runs to about $6 billion each year. War contracts indirectly subsidize countless other industries. It is not my intent to decry governmental aid for food and housing, nor in any manner to compare or equate the values of art with those represented by minerals, oil, shipping. But it would appear that our government considers art of minimal importance for its citizens.

What has all this to do with the movies and their possible future? A great deal. Of all the performing arts, motion pictures are seen by the greatest number of people and exercise the greatest influence on our way of life. If there is to be a concern manifested by the government in aiding any of the arts, motion pictures should be singled out for special attention. Their potential share of the National Endowment allotment would be a pittance at best. The only way to advance film as an art form in America would be by some form of government subsidization. Such a donation *should* be made for films alone, completely disassociated from any other category of art.

It is important to indicate clearly and immediately that this proposed subsidization for films should *not* be for the majority of Hollywood films. There is certainly no reason to underwrite the second-rate film which is Hollywood's mainstay. These should take their chances in the market place as any other factory product does. But since the film industry —unlike any other manufacturer of salable commodities—is capable of a tremendous and vital contribution to our humanistic environment, those members of the film community who want to embark on ventures of cultural benefit should be able to do so, independent of the profit system.

Needless to say, Hollywood is not all of a piece. Not everyone in Hollywood is a Philistine. It has always been a haven for talented people as well—people devoted to film as an art form. It is these dedicated film-makers who should be sustained by the national government. Those members of the industry emboldened to make films of quality and maturity for a limited but discriminating audience, who have proven their ability to do so, should be helped. Their films could be sold and released by the major companies to assure the widest possible distribution, but the essential protective point is that at least a proportion of their costs should be defrayed from federal sources. That such productions would expose and encourage new and exciting talent in every aspect of film-making would be an additional and gratuitous benefit for the public as well as for the industry.

This is not as radical a concept as might appear. Many countries—France, England, Japan, Italy, Sweden, among others—have seen the wisdom of stimulating the production of films, first, to be sure, for their commercial values, but also, and significantly, for their aesthetic values, and because they serve as cultural ambassadors. These countries have recognized films as the single new art development that transcends language barriers.

American films have been accused of intellectual sterility, slavish devotion to formulas, lack of imagination, indifference to aesthetic values, degrading capitulation to commercialism, blatant disregard of discriminating tastes, deliberate pandering to vulgarity, and emphasis on arbitrary violence. These are all familiar pejoratives in our critical press, and the continued popularity of the imported film as a standard of comparison has underlined the truth of these indictments.

Czechoslovakia, Mexico, India, Japan, France, Italy, England, Germany, are frequently praised for producing motion pictures of a higher quality than those made by Hollywood. What is often forgotten is that we see only a small percentage of the hundreds of films produced abroad. The average commercial film made in Europe or India or Japan or Mexico is as trite and mindless as any comparable Hollywood offering. The American cinema has no monopoly on mediocrity: Europe and Asia have their own creative shortcomings. But it is important to remember that many of the foreign films we *do* see, screened and selected though they are from among many hundreds, *are* frequently outstandingly creative. Bosley Crowthers, for many years film critic of the *New York Times*, said: "Experience has long since prepared us to accept the uncomfortable fact that the best work in motion pictures—the most intelligent, progressive, astute, and alert to what is happening to people—is being done abroad." Crowthers is right. But why is this so?

Does the fault lie with our movie makers? Are they all really inferior to their European competitors? Are Hollywood technicians wanting in ingenuity? Are there no writers and producers and directors and performers in Hollywood who are unafraid to be challenging and innovative? The answers are obvious. There is no cinema magic which is uniquely foreign. A number of our creators and craftsmen are fully as gifted as their foreign counterparts, *if granted the opportunity to display their talents.* What prevents this? Why are a number of foreign films superior to those made in Hollywood?

Apart from subsidization, which is by far the most important reason, there are various explanations—many of which have to do with differences in the structure of the industry in Hollywood and Europe. Many of these differences have been explored already, but they merit repetition:

1. The cost of producing a film in many foreign countries is considerably lower than it would be in America.

2. Although the contemporary American censorship code is not even a "useful fraud" (so called by Stanley Kauffmann in *The New Republic*), it is still restrictive and has no analogue in foreign lands. Moreover, America, unlike Europe, is faced with local censorship proscriptions from literally hundreds of villages, towns, and cities as well as many states, plus powerful pressure groups and lobbies which impede critical portrayals of various professions, industries, and minority groups.

3. Television exercises a baleful influence on American films, an influence which is barely existent overseas thus far. One way or another, very few pictures are being made nowadays in America without serious consideration of their potential sales value to television. When films are so conceived, they almost necessarily become debased.

4. American films are apt to be subject to multiple controls through committee supervision (usually by men unversed in film-making). In Europe the one-man film (usually the product of the director) is the work of a single individual who is accorded creative autonomy.

5. Stars dominate American films. Outside of the United

States stars are also valuable commodities, but a large number of foreign films ignore this factor and are conceived and presented without marquee personalities.

6. American film companies, especially now, are part of a gigantic financial complex, publicly owned by stockholders whose profit anticipations must be satisfied. Although there are exceptions (a number of American companies have invested in various European productions), most foreign films are either owned by one man or by a small private corporation.

There are other differences between the foreign and the domestic film industries, but the most basic, most influential, and most potent cause of the superiority of the better foreign films can be ascribed to subsidization. Foreign films are often subsidized in part by outright grants to encourage indigenous production. France, England, Italy, Sweden, and Spain have institutions through which the producer is helped to finance his film. His risk is thus calculably diminished at the outset. These subsidies either come from the government directly or from organizations of a semi-official nature.

In France an annual fund is derived from the imposition of a fixed tax of a little less than a franc on every ticket sold at the box office. Each picture ultimately receives approximately fourteen percent of the producer's share of the income collected from this taxation process. Therefore, the producer with a box-office success will receive more money than the one whose picture has failed to attain audience approval. The sum is given to the producer as a credit to be applied to his next production, thus providing him with the assurance that he can plan for the future. Similar financial assistance is also given to short subjects (money prizes are awarded to a maximum of fifty each year), thus encouraging film apprenticeship which has been a proving ground for such luminaries as Jean-Luc Godard, François Truffaut,

Alain Resnais, and Louis Malle, to name but a few. The New Wave of French productions could never have come into being without this financial sponsorship.

England, too, supports its national film-makers under the aegis of the Eady Plan. The cinematograph Film Act of 1957 expressly provides for the proceeds of a theater ticket tax to be used in subsidizing British films. This levy is administered by the British Film Fund Agency, which divides the money among producers in relation to the box-office success of their respective productions. This has averaged for some producers 40 percent or more on earnings and has gone as high as 55 percent.

Japan also has a national program in which modest amounts are donated to those producers who sponsor films specifically designed for the taste and enlightenment of the younger generation, that is, experimental films. A study is now being made in Japan of additional grants on $5,556,000 for the industry in the form of an annual subsidy for three years.

Spanish films are underwritten with a grant of 15 percent of the gross profits of national films, and the percentage occasionally goes as high as 30 percent for films of outstanding excellence. The Film Aid Fund supervising these gifts also maintains a school for film trainees and makes annual awards to individual pictures ranging from $33,400 to $75,150—sums which are often equal to nearly half the total cost of a Spanish film. There are also subsidies for directors who create films of "artistic interest."

Italy, too, assists its film-makers, with 13 percent of the gross earnings of a film in the first five years it is shown. The Italians also finance a production school, the Centro Sperimentale, and distribute annual awards of $64,000 each to films demonstrating "special or artistic qualifications." Lesser sums are awarded to meritorious short subjects.

Holland's films are financed in part by the Netherlands Production Fund, controlled jointly by the Holland Cinema League and the government. A producer may receive $30,000 to $100,000, depending on the viability of the production he envisages and the amount of his own capital. This grant is in the form of a loan to be repaid from his box-office receipts, but with no penalty if such receipts are not forthcoming.

Sweden furthers film production through the Swedish Film Institute, which awards a series of cash bonuses to "good" pictures selected by a committee of educators, psychologists, film critics, and industry representatives. Of the money collected from a levy of 10 percent of the box-office receipts from all pictures, one-third goes to the Swedish National Film School for experimental films and the training of future film-makers, one-third to box-office winners in proportion to the number of tickets sold, and the last third to films which lost money but won recognition or awards for excellence.

Other countries that donate money to promote national film production include India and Denmark, the latter donating $184,720 annually for feature films and $32,589 for short subjects. West Germany provides $1 million dollars every year in film subsidies supplemented by various federal film prizes, and also supports the Association For Young Film Makers.

It is undeniable that the intent of most of these subsidizations is to foster film-making in general, whether commercial or artistic. And it is obvious, particularly in England and France, that subsidization benefits accrue to the individual producer in direct proportion to his competence in making pictures that are profitable at the box office. In short, European subsidies are by no means devoid of commercialism, but it should be noted that a very considerable number of the awards, prizes, loans, gifts, donations, and grants are offered to film schools, apprenticeship programs, experimental films, films of outstanding excellence, films of artistic interest, films which lost money at the box office but won recognition for merit, films which possess cultural assets, and so forth. In essence, while it is true that all these countries distribute a sizeable portion of their largesse to promote films as an industry, they also make deliberate provisions for the nourishment of films as an art. Even the commercial filmmaker who receives his grant for a box-office success is thereby encouraged to gamble, as the result of just such a grant, on a film which he has long wanted to make but which he deems noncommercial. The grant assures him that his investment is partially guaranteed and protected. Depending on the amount of money he receives, he has the privilege of making a film without total dependence on the vagaries of box-office returns for its and his survival.

Subsidized films are not necessarily films of quality and distinction; every film is the product of individual talent and ability. But for those foreign film-makers who cherish film as an art form, subsidization allows them to undertake projects which would be financially indefensible in America. In our country no one can afford to make films only for the discriminating few. Our cost structure makes such ventures too financially hazardous. Selective subsidization of some kind, in the future, might be one, if not the only answer to those critics who excoriate the low cultural level of our cinema, an answer that would differentiate between the average light, entertaining or trite Hollywood production and a variable percentage of quality films to be made within the framework of Hollywood, but partially free of Hollywood's obligations.

Nor need such subsidization be confined to Hollywood. There is an exciting corps of dedicated film-makers outside Hollywood, many from the various colleges and universities now offering film courses, a number of whom might merit federal assistance. If this now neglected substratum of new talent were added to the creative talent already in Hollywood and granted financial assistance, a number of distinguished films might evolve.

Subsidization for American films in an attempt to raise the level of creativity is not as innovative an idea as might be assumed; it has been advanced from many quarters for some years. Arthur Mayer, a motion picture historian and a veteran exhibitor, wrote in the *Producer's Journal*, "Worthy people constantly complain about the low intellectual and artistic standard of a large percentage of our motion pictures. Unless we adopt a system of film subsidies as practiced by European governments, this condition will continue to exist." George Bernard Shaw, quoted in Richard Dyer MacCann's *Film And Society*, said: "The moral is, of course, that the State should endow the cinema, as it should endow all forms of art to the extent necessary to place its highest forms above the need for competition."

The National Association of Theater Owners, a powerful group of exhibitors, has established a special committee to investigate the feasibility of a film production subsidy; and not too long ago the Screen Actors Guild urged the industry "to give immediate and sincere attention to the possibilities of establishing such a plan [subsidization] for American production within our geographical borders."

The inauguration of the American Film Institute under the auspices of the National Foundation on the Arts and Humanities Act of 1965, with George Stevens, Jr., as its director, is the first institutional acknowledgement of America's delinquency in treating film as an art form. Its five-pronged program for training, education, production, publications, and archival activities is heartening. Certainly it is the nearest approach ever made in America to a national film school such as has existed for many years in various European countries where acting, writing, directing, editing, photography, producing, music, and art direction are taught. Unfortunately, its operations are presently limited to only three years and its budget of $5,200,000 (two-thirds of which came from the Ford Foundation and the Motion Picture Association of America) is pathetically small. In 1971 the National Endowment granted it an additional $1,000,000, but this is still far from adequate for its extensive program of activities. Nor is its budget automatically renewable.

There would, of course, be problems in any federal subsidization, the most significant one being the composition of the adjudicating tribunal: who decides which productions should be helped? But such a committee could be selected from among public spirited citizens with recommendatory powers to the government, or from officials of the government itself, men and women chosen from various professions —educators, statesmen, critics, psychologists, sociologists, philosophers, cinema experts—a directorate similar to the one in Sweden. It would be the task of such a council to evaluate film projects and base its grants on the potential merit of each submission.

For those who think that subvention could lead to subversion, there is an alternate avenue of assistance. This would be from the American film industry itself. Hollywood might reflect on the advisability of channeling a specific portion of its dollar gains (assuming there will be gains in the future!) from commercially successful films into a fund for more experimental ventures, rather than seek outside bounty. The major companies could install a system of self-taxation, the proceeds to be utilized for the sponsorship and development of art films. It would be ironic if Hollywood's skill in producing the commonplace were to provide funds for filmmaking on a more artistic level; ironic, indeed, if Hollywood could be its own Maecenas.

The potential advantages of such a self-imposed undertaking are self-evident, for it is only by trying the untried that any art form remains alive. To liberate our more conscientious film-makers from having to reenforce the low level of taste of the general public might permit them slowly to attract new and larger audiences as greater numbers became exposed to films of quality in their neighborhood theaters. This would not only be a giant leap forward in our cultural progression, it might even become a profitable investment in the long run. As Charles Champlin observed in the *Los Angeles Times* (April 24, 1972), "To say that movies succeed by quality rather than kind is almost useless as guidance, but in the end it may be the one abiding truth."

Whatever Hollywood's future, its present is in a dolorous state. If subsidization of some kind is not forthcoming, the portents for Hollywood are dim. Unless some redemptive effort is made to infuse art into films, Hollywood will remain a place of hazardous commercial enterprise purveying mediocre entertainment, a fountainhead of the trivial and the trifling.

Hollywood has been described as "the sleeping giant of the arts." Whether the "sleeping giant" will ever be awakened to his full powers is impossible to say, but the potentialities are there. Whether the movies will remain "an eruption of trash that has lamed the American mind and retarded Americans from becoming cultured people," as Ben Hecht said, or whether the "popularity of motion pictures will ride higher and higher as the quality of motion pictures rises higher and higher," as D. W. Griffith prophesied, is for Hollywood itself to determine.

SELECTED
BIBLIOGRAPHY

ARNHEIM, RUDOLF. *Film As Art*. Berkeley and Los Angeles: University of California Press, 1967.

BATTCOCK, GREGORY, ed. *The New American Cinema*. New York: E. P. Dutton & Co., 1967.

BOBKER, LEE R. *The Elements of Film*. New York: Harcourt Brace & World Inc., 1969.

DAY, BETH. *This Was Hollywood*. New York: Doubleday and Company, 1960.

DE MILLE, WILLIAM. *Hollywood Saga*. New York: E. P. Dutton & Co., 1939.

FISCHER, EDWARD. *The Screen Arts*. New York: Sheed and Ward, 1960.

GEDULD, HARRY M., ed. *Film Makers on Film Making*. Bloomington: Indiana University Press, 1967.

GOODMAN, EZRA. *The Fifty Year Decline and Fall of Hollywood*. New York: Simon and Schuster, 1961.

GREEN, ABEL, ed. *The Spice of Variety*. New York: Henry Holt and Company, 1952.

GREEN, ABEL, and JOE LAURIE. *Show Biz: Variety from Vaude to Video*. New York: Henry Holt and Company, 1951.

HAMBLETT, CHARLES. *The Hollywood Cage*. New York: Hart Publishing Company, 1969.

HIGHAM, CHARLES, and JOEL GREENBERG. *Hollywood in the Forties*. New York: A. S. Barnes, 1968.

HOUSTON, PENELOPE. *The Contemporary Cinema*. Baltimore: Penguin Books, 1963.

JACOBS, LEWIS. *The Rise of the American Film: A Critical History.* New York: Harcourt Brace and Company, 1939.

KNIGHT, ARTHUR. *The Liveliest Art.* New York: The Macmillan Company, 1957.

LAWSON, JOHN HOWARD. *Film in the Battle of Ideas.* New York: Masses and Midstream, 1953.

———. *Film: The Creative Process.* New York: Hill and Wang, 1964.

MAC CANN, RICHARD DYER. *Hollywood in Transition.* Boston: Houghton Mifflin and Company, 1962.

———. *Film and Society.* New York: Charles Scribner's Sons, 1964.

MAC GOWAN, KENNETH. *Behind the Screen.* New York: Dell Publishing Company, 1965.

MANVELL, ROGER. *New Cinema in the USA.* New York: E. P. Dutton & Co., 1968.

MAYERSBURG, PAUL. *Hollywood: The Haunted House.* New York: Ballantine Books, 1967.

MONTAGU, IVOR. *Film World.* London: Pelican Books, 1964.

POWDERMAKER, HORTENSE. *Hollywood: The Dream Factory.* Boston: Little Brown & Company, 1950.

RAGAWAY, MARTIN. "A Hollywood Dictionary." *Variety* (December, 1951). Reprinted in Abel Green, ed. *The Spice of Variety.* New York: Henry Holt and Company, 1952.

RENAN, SHELDON. *An Introduction to the American Underground Film.* New York: E. P. Dutton & Co., 1967.

RIVKIN, ALLEN, and LAURA KERR. *Hello, Hollywood!* New York: Doubleday & Company, 1962.

ROSENBERG, BERNARD, and DAVID MANNING WHITE, eds. *Mass Culture: The Popular Arts in America.* Glencoe, Ill.: The Free Press, 1957.

ROSTEN, LEO. *Hollywood: The Movie Colony—The Movie Makers.* New York: Harcourt Brace and Company, 1941.

SAMUELS, CHARLES THOMAS. *A Casebook on Film.* New York: Van Nostrand Reinhold Company, 1970.

SELDES, GILBERT. *The 7 Lively Arts.* New York: Harper & Brothers, 1924.

———. *The Movies Come from America.* New York: Charles Scribner's Sons, 1964.

———. *The Great Audience.* New York: Viking Press, 1950.

STEPHENSON, RALPH, and J. R. DEBRIX. *The Cinema As Art.* Baltimore: Penguin Books, 1965.

TALBOT, DANIEL, ed. *Film: An Anthology.* Berkeley and Los Angeles: University of California Press, 1967.

INDEX